Glasgow-the first 800 years

By Hugh Cochrane

Foreword

Glasgow has produced many things, including books about itself. In recent years people in Britain and abroad have asked for a short account of its history until the present time. This book has been written to fulfil that purpose.

Glasgow-the first 800 years

A copy of what is believed to be the first seal of the city. It was in use in 1325.

Glasgow made the River Clyde, changed it from a shallow, meandering stream, filled with trout and salmon, to a great commercial highway and a row of shipyards that put half the world to sea.

1 *The old bridge at the Broomielaw.*
2 *The Georgian elegance of Carlton Place in the days when the Clyde there was usually less than two feet deep.*
3 *One of the earliest steamships, passing the Broomielaw.*
4 *'Clyde-built', in the heyday of shipbuilding, stood not only for skill and service but versatility—from warships to cargo liners to the true poetry of the shipbuilder, the steam yacht.*

Glasgow had no birthright. It is a self-made city, conceived with almost no natural advantages or the patronage of princes. It is a self-made city, nourished by the strength and, more important, the adaptability of generations of its people.

In the beginning there was no good reason for it, even by primitive standards. A fort, an undependable ford, and a church, from which a saintly man proclaimed: 'Let Glasgow flourish.' Against most of the rules of human settlement, it did flourish; not exclusively perhaps through the preaching of the Word, as he had commended, but through a stubborn kind of human endeavour that demanded its place in the world.

The aggressive pride of the self-made remains one of the characteristics of the city. If its validity was put to the test and the fundamental question asked, 'Why Glasgow?', the inevitable answer would be a defiant growl of 'Why not?'

Neither monks nor merchants would have made a prospectus on it at the start. Who would take pilgrims or trade to a place stuck out on the north-west corner of the fringe of Europe? The Celts, who had called it 'Glasghu' or the 'dear, green place', were savages from a bleak, wooded country who could scarcely fashion the crudest canoes. The Romans, who knew more about green and salient places, had little time for it.

Less than 2000 years later Glasgow had become the second city of a larger empire than the Romans had known. Within its bounds, it could support more than a million people—the most northerly city in the world ever to attain a population of a million—and still export enough people to ensure that its skills and its products and its character were universally known.

The people who formed that character were primarily Lowland Scots later inter-mixed with the Highlanders and immigrant Irish whom the city absorbed. They fused together elements of stubbornness, some ingenuity and a prodigious amount of adaptability.

Glasgow, since it first assumed any geographical identity, has had to adapt. As a place on the colder edge of Europe, it first made its trade with the world and only then created within itself a port where no natural port had previously existed. And when the tides of mercantile trade turned against it, the city went on to build ships for the traffic of other nations and to become a major instrument of the industrial revolution.

The River Clyde did not make the city; the city made the Clyde by sound engineering and hard labour. It put half the world to sea. It stamped its identity in iron on the machines and the locomotives of the new, industrialised countries as well as the old. When its economic prosperity was at its height, it needed no lessons in advertising itself and was totally convinced its name was a byword in every continent. A Glasgow shipowner, answering a complaint from a foreign competitor that he was spreading his empire too far, snapped: 'Being from Glasgow, I can go where I like. I'd open a line to Hell, if I wasn't sure you had an agent there already.'

Set alongside the record of other great cities of the world, its relative standing as a manufacturing and trading centre has declined in the past generation or two. But its history illustrates that this has happened in previous centuries and there was almost invariably a subsequent upsurge in its fortunes. It has always maintained an alert appetite for fresh opportunities, new technologies. Once its people made their living from fish, timber and hides; then there were textiles and tobacco; and, in the past two centuries, steel, ships and machines. Adaptation still continues. Not long ago an American economist said that Clydesiders are the Junkers of the trade of Europe—'They will beat you yet....'

At its lowest definition, it is perhaps a civic instinct for self-preservation. Certainly, that obtained in the times of bloody change centuries ago when Scotland was frequently an embattled kingdom, and it obtains now in the role that is being set for Glasgow in the economic re-vitalisation of Scotland. It was typified by the ironclad rules laid down by the guilds of craftsmen and merchants to guard the city's livelihood and by the firmness with which their civic leaders refused to have any truck with the armies of Bonnie Prince Charlie, who could extract from Glasgow only £14,000, a mistress and one drunken shoemaker to join the ranks of his rebellion.

In the tapestry of the city's history, the beginnings of which are vague and debatable, there are only a few internationally renowned figures—such as James Watt,

5

the inventor, and Adam Smith, the philosopher and economist, who may be said to have directly influenced its status and development. But it is a tapestry enlivened in parts by dramatic and violent episodes of mercantile adventure, religious strife, and civil uprising. The dominant, though not commonly recognisable figures, who stride across it are entrepreneurs, statesmen and administrators.

The incidental, passing parade of the famous includes Mary, Queen of Scots, who came to witness her final military defeat at Glasgow; Robert Burns, who came courting; Chopin, who came apparently against his will to play the piano, and many more. There are Daniel Defoe, Doctor Samuel Johnson, Sir Walter Scott, Wordsworth, Gladstone and others in an historical procession of the famous and infamous; there are soldiers, engineers, scientists, architects, revolutionaries, a plethora of neglected geniuses and forgotten eccentrics, and a rogues' gallery of extraordinary and long-remembered murderers.

Philosophers and literateurs have not achieved such durable recognition from Glasgow as it has accorded to men of action and men who made money. It has never had an artists' quarter or any effete fraction. As a place for the hard-headed and fiercely practical, it has always had big plans in the offing, big projects on the stocks.

Now the scale of them is bigger than ever. As the obstructive relics of the industrial revolution and its by-product of teeming tenements are banished, the overcrowding is being eased, the commercial centre of the city is being re-shaped, and the urban motorways zoom north and south, east and west, trailing their dusty slipstream of controversy. Adaptability shows itself again, and Glasgow has learned that there is no adaptation without acrimony. But it is more than just the sum of bricks and mortals. It is the great economic heart of Scotland.

The place at 55° 51' North and 4° 17' West is no mere city.

If you would measure the evolution of a community that is founded beside a river, there is a simple and appropriate criterion in the history and scale of its bridges. They are a changing index of the traffic of people and goods, and, to some extent, the fortunes of a town or city.

In the passing of a thousand years, there were the ancient timber footbridges, replaced by sturdily arched bridges of stone, which could bear horse-drawn vehicles. Later, there were more elegant structures with marble balustrades and wider, smoother concourses; and bridges built higher to allow the passage of bigger ships beneath them; and bridges built stronger to carry railways. Old ones are demolished and mourned. New ones are erected and almost always admired. They are symbols.

The latest of the series of bridges crossing the Clyde near the Centre of Glasgow is the Kingston, a sweeping sky-high motorway. From its great height there is a new and wonderful perspective of the city and its precincts. Towards the fringes there are the vast areas of municipal houses and the industrial estates; and, closer to the centre,

the new hospital buildings, the bulk of the two universities, the high-rise offices, the handsome store of Victorian buildings, and the surprising grace of the public parks, cast around generously like bouquets among the red sandstone and the grey. From this windy, eerie eminence, it is possible with a little imagination to foresee the shape of things to come and at the same time identify some of the oldest landmarks that were known to the first settlers in the dear green place.

Glasgow now stretches for mile upon mile on either side of the river. But for hundreds of years it was sited exclusively on the northern side among the hills of boulder clay, the 'drumlins', that formed the main contours of the area.

The Clyde was an indolent, shallow stream, which came out of the hills of Lanarkshire in the south and meandered round sandbanks and islands before assuming a deeper course about 10 to 14 miles west of Glasgow. It was probably one to two feet deep for most of the year but seasonal flooding of the lowlands on either side was commonplace. It was well provided with salmon and trout.

St. Mungo came out of the east, from the Lothians or Fife. Kentigern was his birth-name and he was the illegitimate son of a princess, Thenaw, who for her pains had been expelled by her father, the king of Northumbria and the Lothians.

The land in which Mungo settled was part of the kingdom of Strathclyde, stretching from Cumbria to the hills just north of the Clyde. The seat of power was in the fortress of Dumbarton, a steep rock commanding the opening of the estuary, and the kings maintained a palace at Pert Nech (Partick, now part of Glasgow), near the point where the River Kelvin flows into the Clyde.

Mungo, for his part, chose to reside further east, building his church, of wood and wattles, on a high bluff above the Molendinar, another tributary of the Clyde. He was a young man. According to legend, he was only 25 when he was consecrated as a bishop about the year 543. Christianity by then had already achieved a fairly diverse penetration of Scotland, mostly imported from Ireland through the ancient kingdoms of Dalriada and Strathclyde in the west.

The early churches drew people around them. Stories of the teaching and the exploits of their founders were rumoured abroad like a primitive form of community advertising. They gained prestige not only for their erudition, particularly their written works, but their miracles.

A vast folklore of somewhat worldly miracles was created around Mungo. It was said of him that he caused the waters of the River Forth to part. When the King of Strathclyde, Morken, in a fit of royal disapproval, kicked the saint's posterior, the foot which delivered the blow was stricken with gout. Mungo departed to live for some time in Wales, returning after Morken had been succeeded by Rhydderch as King of Strathclyde.

Perhaps his most celebrated, minor miracle was effected for the benefit of Rhydderch's queen, Langueth. A ring, a gift from her husband, had been secretly presented by the queen to her lover. But it had been lost in the Clyde and now the king was demanding to see it on her hand. When the queen in desperation took her problem to the saint, he commanded a fisherman to cast his line or net into the river. A fish was pulled out and in its mouth was the ring.

The fish and the ring are depicted in the city's coat of arms, together with other mementoes of Mungo, a tree, a bird, and a bell, each associated with legends about him. The bell represents a gift from the Pope. The saint is said to have made several journeys to Rome, a tough and hazardous undertaking from what, in those days, must have been the farthest frontiers of the Church. He was an energetic and resolute man, who drew many people to him in Glasgow and founded satellite ministries elsewhere in Scotland.

In the year 601 he died at an advanced age. He was succeeded by one of his disciples, Baldred, who had established a religious settlement near Renfrew, to the west of Glasgow.

The path of history after that is obscured by the confused and blood-stained spoor of tribal and civil wars which raged backwards and forwards across Scotland for three or four centuries. The Picts, the Scots, the Britons, and the invading Danes and Norsemen fought with each other; alliances were created and sundered; loyalties and royalties were as perishable as territorial boundaries. Yet somehow, in the maelstrom of changes in culture and language which accompanied this, the Church was maintained. It certainly kept its place on that hill above the Molendinar in Glasgow.

Regularly under assault from nearly all sides, the Kingdom of Strathclyde was destroyed around the middle of the tenth century. But by then Scotland was becoming unified. The warring incursions of the Norsemen had helped to achieve a form of unity out of expediency and the need for mutual defence. A single and all-powerful kingship was established over Scotland. Gradually, the people's attention turned away from the Norse to their relations with the larger kingdom to the south, England.

Cultural, religious, and political influences slowly filtered into Scotland from the south; some might say they were implanted deliberately. Towards the end of the eleventh century many English refugees from the Norman conquerors settled in Scotland.

The king at that time was Malcolm, who was seraphically henpecked. His queen was Margaret, of the royal house of Wessex, a pious and erudite woman who apparently had a formidable capacity for getting her own way. The Church, which was an assortment of different practices, from the near primitive to the orthodox Roman, assumed greater cohesion and spiritual lustre under her guidance. While her husband blundered through a series of political misadventures and military expeditions, she also dabbled in other kinds of reform. The nobles were encouraged to eat off individual metal plates. Silks and fine cloths were imported. Manners and fashion were elevated. Margaret tried to bring a woman's touch to an unkempt hovel of a kingdom.

The civilising processes, fostered by her, were developed further by her three sons when they, in turn, gained the throne. Town life came into being, there was the beginning of regular trade with other parts of Britain, the country minted its own coins, and the Church grew under royal patronage.

King David I, who helped to restore the see of Glasgow around 1115, became king in 1124, and he is generally accredited with conferring the first burgh charters, the formal recognition of towns. But Glasgow was not one of them. They were mostly in the east of Scotland and were places with harbours or important river crossings.

Glasgow was still a hamlet. St. Mungo's original church became the site of a cathedral, built of stone and wood, consecrated in the presence of King David in 1136. Around it were the dwellings of the bishop, the clergy, their dependants and servants. The river crossing was of little importance. Between it and the cathedral there probably were a handful of crude cottages, occupied by the families of fishermen and perhaps some masons and wrights. Records of the time are scarce, but there is little evidence of metal-working or cloth-making, which were practised in other parts of the country. A papal writ of 1161, defining the tithes (taxes) payable to the diocese of Glasgow, listed grain, wool, lint, butter, lambs, goats, and poultry as the produce.

The man who put Glasgow on the map was a political genius called Bishop Jocelin. He came out of the Border country, a part of Britain frequently riven by sectional intrigues and armed battles, and it is perhaps an instinct for survival, acquired there, that was accountable for his success.

Jocelin, a Cistercian, was Abbot of Melrose. In 1174, he was elected Bishop of Glasgow, and he was consecrated in the following year. He lost no time in putting pressure on the king, who was then William the Lion.

William was in need of friends and money. In 1174, he had made an abortive attack on Northumbria, which had ended in his capture at Alnwick. With his feet reportedly tied together under the belly of a horse, he had been taken to Henry II of England at Northampton and then sent to prison at Falaise in Normandy. Several months later, he had been released after pledging, among other concessions, the surrender of Scottish sovereignty to English overlordship.

As a means of re-establishing himself, he encouraged the spread of feudalism because knights and their followers could represent military support for him. He bestowed burgh charters because he needed the corporate strength of the traders and craftsmen in towns; and he needed the rents. (He was later to redeem the pledge of Scottish sovereignty on payment of 10,000 merks to finance Richard the Lion Heart of England in the Crusades.)

Glasgow became a burgh of barony. The feudal superior was the Bishop, who was given powers to appoint

burgesses, usually landowners or traders. He also appointed magistrates or burgh officers of his choice or from a list of nominees offered by the burgesses. A burgh of barony had privileges of trading but they were usually not as extensive as those granted to royal burghs.

Authority was given to the Bishop (and his successors) to hold a market each Thursday. In later years Jocelin obtained from William the right to hold a fair for a prescribed period each July and, 800 years afterwards, this is still traditionally recognised as the Glasgow holiday.

To judge from the simple, known facts of his life, Jocelin must have been a dynamic force in the early growth of the town and his diplomatic or political prowess rather suggests that when his hands were not together in the posture of prayer he was making sure that the left one did not know what the right one was doing. He was a worldly man, who played the king against the Church and vice-versa.

Part of his motivation in procuring a burgh charter in the first place was probably to guarantee a source of funds for maintaining his cathedral. When it was destroyed by fire, some time in the late 1180s, he was dedicated and forceful in enlisting support to re-build it. One of his enterprises was to hire a namesake, Jocelin, a monk of Furness Abbey, in Lancashire. Now Brother Jocelin was a biographer of saints. He had already scripted St. Patrick and some others with colourful detail. His new subject: a life of St. Mungo, which would be copied and preached abroad in the diocese, thus inspiring adherents to contribute to the re-building of the cathedral. The work, copiously invested with stories of miracles, survived remarkably well.

Bishop Jocelin was much favoured by a succession of three Popes. For a man in the relative wilds of north-west Europe he received an extraordinary number of Papal missives from Rome. In 1198, he even succeeded in getting the excommunication of William the Lion revoked, thanks to his personal overtures in the Holy City.

In 1197, the new cathedral of Glasgow was dedicated and opened by Jocelin. Less than two years later he died. Part of the present building is generally considered to date from his time.

The stone masons and craftsmen were probably among the main supporters of the weekly market in the town. In those days it was fairly common for them to hawk their goods and rent out their services alongside the sellers of vegetables, fish and hides. As the town grew, the market became more important and from it new avenues of trade were opened to other parts of Scotland.

Outsiders became hostile. In particular, Rutherglen, which had become a burgh 50 years before Glasgow, and Dumbarton, the former capital of Strathclyde, which achieved burgh status after Glasgow. Both of these were royal burghs with, nominally at least, superior rights of trading. There were frequent disputes with them about tolls and the passage of goods. But Glasgow successfully resisted their interference with its commerce, although a bitter rivalry with Dumbarton was to persist for hundreds of years.

The population in the 13th century could be described as ecclesiastical camp followers in the main. They were fringe dwellers around a great cathedral, a pattern of community living that could be found in England, France, or Italy at that time. The bishops were a succession of men of Norman blood, drawing rents from nearly all of the most fertile lands in the area. It is in this period that the first magistrates and civil courts are recorded, and the earliest provosts or leaders of the town council were also men of Norman blood.

Throughout Europe there was a clear improvement in the living standards of the ordinary people, although in the west of Scotland the degree of improvement was far less. The War of Independence, resulting from the reassertion of English overlordship by King Edward I, had lasting, harmful consequences nearly everywhere.

William Wallace, who roused the Scots to rebellion after English armies had conquered most of the country, came from Elderslie, near Glasgow. A towering figure, both in physique and reputation, he led guerrilla campaigns against the invaders. According to some popular accounts of history he fought a battle against them in Glasgow and it was in Glasgow at a later date that he was betrayed and captured before being taken to London for execution. But reliable records are few, partly because of the sacking, looting and general upheaval which accompanied that war.

King Edward helped himself to Glasgow's resources when he visited the English garrison in the city around 1300-01. He commandeered the castle, which had been built as the home of the bishops, and appropriated timber for the construction of battle wagons.

The battle wagons and ponderous English war machine finally trundled to disaster in soggy ground at Bannockburn in 1314. Robert the Bruce, who had led the victorious Scottish army, became king. But it did not bring peace and stability to the country for long.

The development of many towns, such as Glasgow, had been blighted by the effects of the protracted, if spasmodic, war. It took them many years to recover. A generation or so after Bannockburn, when the Scots and English were yet again in armed conflict, a severe epidemic of plague killed probably more people in the towns than the numbers that took the field in that battle.

The history of Glasgow in the century after the ravages of the Black Death is poorly documented. Judging by the rise in its offerings to the coffers of the Great Chamberlain of Scotland in the late 1300s, its commercial traffic was picking up again. The religious community continued to be augmented. Not far from the cathedral, a second monastery was founded when the Franciscans came to join the Dominicans, who had been in the town for about two centuries. In those days, they were the chief traders and even money lenders, a practice which seems to have been more common in Scotland than among their more sternly disciplined brethren in England.

The Church needed manpower. Its hold over the area around Glasgow was even stronger and its revenues from feus, trade, and probably dispensations were lucrative. The two main pillars of the Church were St. Andrews and Glasgow. Their rivalry made it inevitable that when St. Andrews established a university, as it did in 1412, Glasgow should follow suit. That took some time. Glasgow University was eventually founded in 1451.

Pope Nicholas V, although with spreading Lollardy and political intrigues in Europe he must have had other things on his mind, was kind to Glasgow. He placed it in a category above most other universities, which tended to offer a narrow, even specialist range of learning. The Papal Bull ordained it to be ' a studium generale, wherein might flourish theology, canon and civil law, as well as the arts and any other lawful faculty'. Nicholas modelled its constitution on that of his own alma mater, the University of Bologna.

The first chancellor was Bishop William Turnbull and the dominant purpose was the training of clergy. Classes at the start appear to have been conducted in the crypt of the cathedral. Later the university obtained its own premises on the east side of the High Street.

Did it succeed in attracting students? There is conflicting evidence about this; but it was certainly slow in attracting any academic fame. God and Mammon were served, directly and indirectly. Priests were produced and the presence of a university not only gave the town a new status symbol but stimulated its enlargement. Within 50 years a significant number of new buildings had been erected in its vicinity. The town was beginning to attain a recognisable shape.

Around the same time as the founding of the university, it had been raised to the status of a burgh of regality. The powers of the Bishop were extended by this new charter. Certain lands owned by the royal household were gifted to him and his successors.

Scotland was now ruled by the Stuart monarchs. To a large extent, their whole dynasty was characterised by conflict and disaster. The country was unstable, woefully slow, by comparison with England, in evolving constitutional government. There was strife among the nobles and recurring battles with the English. Fortunately for Glasgow, it did not suffer much from the direct effects of fighting.

A visitor to the town in the latter part of the 15th century, John Hardyng, took a liking to it. He had been sent as a rather superior spy by the English royal household, who wanted to find certain deeds or other documents to be used in proving their sovereignty over Scotland. Hardying, who took about half a lifetime to complete the job, reported (in verse, for some obscure reason) to Edward IV, and described Glasgow as:

> 'A good cytee and universitee
> Where plentifull is the countrie
> Also replenished well with all commoditie.'

James IV, who was King of Scotland, took pleasure in the growth of urban life. He was also known for his fondness for European culture and, with the mental adventurousness of the Renaissance man perhaps, for artillery. It is recorded that when he visited Glasgow in 1497 he gave three shillings to the poor folk of the place and sixteen shillings to the man who guided him to Stirling that night. Yet in the same year he paid thirteen shillings for minstrels to provide musical accompaniment for the passage of his new gun, 'Mons Meg', down the hill at Edinburgh Castle, where, incidentally, it still stands. His sense of priorities, like his military judgement, seems to have been execrable.

The poor of Glasgow were probably not as numerous or as badly off as those in some of the larger burghs. There was plenty of work in other activities besides fishing and agriculture. There was simple processing, such as the barrelling of herring and ale, and many more goods were being made from hides. The working week was close to a full seven days, except for time off for religious observances and occasional feast days.

Most of the ordinary people spoke a Scots vernacular version of English, although the Gaelic language probably persisted in Glasgow more strongly than in other parts of the Lowlands. A working man dressed in short trousers (usually of coarse, grey cloth); a thick, loose-fitting shirt, and a woollen bonnet. A straight, close-fitting dress, ending above the ankle, was most common among women, and they covered their heads with a rough equivalent of the modern headsquare. For those who could afford them, there were crudely fashioned shoes—feet coverings would be a better term—of untreated skins.

All of Scotland was impoverished by the outcome of the Battle of Flodden in 1513 when thousands of its young men were slaughtered by the English. The breadth of support for the foolhardy James IV caused every community to be afflicted to a greater or lesser degree.

In a country, again beset by the feuds among its own warlords, the hierarchy of royalty, nobility and clergy, and, at the lowest level, peasantry was changing. The craftsmen, traders, and the literate non-clerical people were coming through as a middle force.

The town council of Glasgow in 1516 acquired authority to issue seals of cause to crafts, granting them special privileges and exemptions. First to receive this formal recognition were the skinners and furriers, although they had probably maintained a loose, corporate identity for about two centuries. The rules of the craft incorporated standards of admission, regulations about the treatment of apprentices by masters, and rates of payment. The skinners had been lobbying for such recognition for some time. There are signs that their generous funding of a cathedral altar to St. Christopher (their patron saint) in 1514 helped to influence the council, and thereafter it seems to have been a common practice for crafts to appoint and maintain altars.

Next in the queue for seals of cause came the bakers, tailors, hammermen and fleshers. The weavers, who have

Mary, Queen of Scots

Lord Darnley

John Knox

staggered down through history as a particularly drunken company, showed an awareness of their institutional problem at an early stage. In their rules of 1526, it was sternly laid down that the trade deacon and the masters of the craft must not be found drinking at the expense of the guild's funds. The penalty was a fine of 10 merks, forfeiture of office, and disbarment from any other office for life.

They could cut and cobble their own forms of self-government in their workshops or mills, but overall power still resided in the Bishop's Palace. The incumbent there was now an archbishop, courtesy of the Holy See. As if envisaging the shape of things to come, he had placed fortifications around the palace.

Less than a year after the first craft guild had secured recognition in Glasgow, there was an event which was to trigger off much more violent changes in the course of the city's history; Martin Luther nailed his conscience on a door in Wittenberg and the Reformation was coming.

Ideas travelled by sea. Like some wines, they did not always travel well. Scotland had less of the written word, to say nothing of the printed word, than most other European countries. That is why some of the great concepts of the Renaissance and the Reformation reached it late and distorted.

As traffic to and from the mainland of Europe became more frequent, there was a greater variety of travellers. Ideas were spread by word of mouth. They were not just about new teachings, but new processes of manufacture and markets for goods.

By the 1530s Glasgow had regular two-way trade with France, the Netherlands, and even the Baltic. An estate owner named William Elphinstone is generally accredited with starting it, exporting cured salmon and herring and bringing back brandy and salt from France. Later a young aristocrat, Archibald Sym, emerged as a merchant adventurer on an even bigger scale.

Henry VIII of England, who seems to have spent nearly as much time taking umbrage at the Scots as he did in finding faults in his wives, sent a personal note of protest to the Scottish court about the ' poaching ' activities of Glasgow merchants. He did so under pressure from English merchants in foreign trade. It was an inverted tribute to the enterprise of a place with a population estimated at just over 3000.

James V of Scotland had been worried about some of the imports. He lamented to the Pope in 1537 that ' foul teaching ' (by implication, heretical books) was being brought in under cover of other cargoes.

James tended to re-inforce his support for the Church at a time when there was a rising resentment, not so much against its doctrines as its clergy. The ill-feeling was fairly deep-rooted in the west of Scotland. In the late 1530s two young Protestant martyrs were tried in Glasgow and were put to death by burning near the east end of the Cathedral. The city had kept reasonably well clear of the damage caused in many of Scotland's internecine wars but it was now more at risk simply because of the growth of its status, particularly that of its religious and academic communities.

It was ravaged in the feuding that followed the death of James V. The Earl of Arran, who was appointed Regent while the King's daughter, Mary (later Queen of Scots) was still an infant, was considered at the time to have Protestant sympathies. Nobles, opposed to him, occupied the Bishop's Palace, and the Earl's troops beseiged it for about 10 days. They surrendered, apparently after an offer of clemency, but all but a few of them were slaughtered. This action aroused the Earl of Glencairn, who then brought 800 men to do battle with the Regent's forces in an area of open country near the Gallowgate, a road running eastwards from the Cathedral. It was a savage encounter in which an estimated 600 died. The Regent won. He then allowed his men to pillage Glasgow because he believed the civic leaders had favoured his enemies. Houses were looted and destroyed.

If Arran was ruthless, he was in keeping with the violent, destructive spirit of the period. English armies were fighting the Scots, who were supplemented by French troops, in the Borders and on the east coast. There were few lines of military demarcation and few durable loyalties. Some Scots, who favoured the Protestant cause, actively supported the English.

The infant queen, Mary, was in safe custody at Inchmahome Priory on the lovely Lake of Menteith, about 25 miles from Glasgow. Eventually, however, it was thought prudent to take her to Dumbarton where she was put aboard a ship for France.

Arran arranged her marriage to the Dauphin while she was growing up in France, and he was granted a French duchy (Duc de Chatellerault). Meanwhile the baby-faced Earl of Lennox, whom he had vanquished in the palace seige in Glasgow, had been punished for treachery. A year after his defeat, Lennox became the father of a son who was to figure in a brief, mysterious episode in the city's history. His name: Lord Darnley.

The wrath of the reformers was spreading like wildfire. Apart from the clamour for changes in doctrine and practice (more dissemination of the scriptures in English or vernacular, an end to the Latin mass, etc.) they wanted to smoke out the worldly misdeeds of the Church. There was its rapacious taxation to maintain its hierarchy in relative luxury. Scotland was a burning bush and the oracular voice from within it was that of John Knox.

Knox was a determined, courageous, and physically tough man; a preacher and historian who never failed to make himself fiercely explicit. Yet there is some mystery about his formative years.

There is a school of thought that he was a student at Glasgow University. It is known that he was born in Haddington, East Lothian, but his father's family had their roots in Ranfurly, about a dozen miles south west of Glasgow. Some of his kinsmen attended Glasgow University. The list of incorporated students for the year 1522 contains the name, ' Joannes Knox '. Some historians

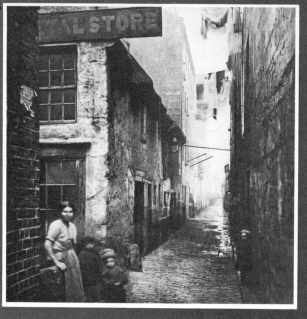

14

Buildings of Glasgow through the centuries.
1 The ancient crypt of the Cathedral where the first classes of the university were held.
2 Provand's Lordship, oldest house in the city, built in 1471.
3 The Old Vennel, off the High Street, as it survived in 1868.
4 One of the last photographs of part of the Gallowgate as its vernacular architecture had looked for about 200 years.
5 An example of one of the better tenements of the 19th century.

believe that the famous reformer, who was born about 1505, could not have been that student.

He was certainly at St. Andrews University as a young man, but that may well have been exclusively as a teacher and not as a student. There are clues in Knox's life, however, which suggest that he was familiar with the city and events which occurred in it. For example, there is his own account of mobbing and fighting in Glasgow Cathedral, which would seem to have happened around 1524 or shortly after that. Well detailed and written with flourishes of Knox's harsh humour, it reads more like an eye-witness report than hearsay. He did not graduate from Glasgow, but he seems to have lived in the city.

Knox was among the leaders of the militant Protestants, who called themselves the Congregation. In 1559, the year in which Mary of Guise (who was then Regent in the absence of her daughter, Mary, Queen of Scots) tried unsuccessfully to suppress them by force, the council of the reformers met in Glasgow. The Duc de Chatellerault, who had promised James Beaton, the Archbishop, that he would protect the Church, changed sides. He joined the Protestant 'Lords of the Congregation', and there is some evidence that he instigated the removal and destruction of idols and decorations from the Cathedral. Mobs wreaked havoc inside the building, although the external features do not appear to have been badly damaged.

The clergy were virtually expelled. Archbishop Beaton was one step ahead of the looters. He transferred holy relics, documents, and ornaments of enormous value from the Cathedral to his fortified palace. In the summer of 1560, one month before the Scottish Parliament accepted the reformed faith as the nation's established religion, he escaped to France with the entire collection.

The inventory of it is startling and too long to itemise. It included relics of value such as the bones of various saints, and parts of the bodies of St. Mungo and Thomas a Becket. Among the archives taken was the original burgh charter of Glasgow. Beaton placed them in the Scots College of Paris and in the Chartreuse there.

Where are they now? Where are the remains of St. Mungo? What happened to them afterwards in Paris is far from clear. It seems probable that many of them were destroyed or removed during the French revolution. Historical records of great value to Glasgow may have been saved from one rebellious mob only to fall victim to another two centuries later.

Not long after Beaton reached Paris, Mary, Queen of Scots, a young widow since the death of the Dauphin, returned to Scotland, a country in which the Parliament was dominated by the new Protestants, the authority of the Pope had been abolished, and her French friends were generally detested. Her mother, Mary of Guise, was dead, and on her first Sunday at home she had to run the gauntlet of an angry crowd to attend a Roman Catholic service in her own chapel. A turbulent reign had begun in earnest.

In the summer of 1565, she married Lord Darnley, the impetuous playboy son of the Earl of Lennox. Darnley, who had been raised in the court of Elizabeth of England, was ambitious. He received the title of King of Scotland under the terms of the 'Crown Matrimonial', but his wife denied him the authority which might accompany it. In the fetid vennel of intrigue that Edinburgh represented in these days, Darnley conspired with the Scots nobles to stage a coup d'etat. David Rizzio, Mary's Italian counsellor, was murdered in her presence at Holyrood Palace. But the plot failed.

Three months later, after their son (who was to become the first king of England and Scotland) had been born, Mary and Darnley had apparently achieved a fragile kind of reconciliation. The child was baptised in the Catholic faith at Stirling Castle on December 17, 1566. But by then Darnley was bitterly at odds with the Queen. When Mary and the child returned to Holyrood Palace he remained at Stirling and then travelled to Glasgow at the end of December.

He stayed in a house in the Drygate district, owned by his father. He was severely ill with what was said to be smallpox, although it was probably another, more violent form of disease (in a contemporary account it was simply 'a great fever of the pox'). What happened to him after that is a series of events which intrigued and divided many historians and biographers.

Mary sent the royal physician to him in January, 1567. But at the same period she was writing to Archbishop Beaton in Paris (where he was now the Scots ambassador) that there were rumours of a plot by Darnley to kidnap his own son and seize the power of government. The rumour had been put about by the Town Clerk of Glasgow.

On or about January 20, Mary travelled to Glasgow with an escort. It was probably risky because she was not popular in the city; the place was rife with kinsmen of Darnley, Lennox Stewarts. However, she stayed for only two or three days and her sole purpose was to remove the sick man to Edinburgh. They did not share the same house while she was in Glasgow. Mary is known to have lived in fairly close proximity during those few days, although the precise address is uncertain. There is a theory that it was Provand's Lordship, which still stands as the oldest house in Glasgow.

Darnley was persuaded, one way or another, that he should be taken to Edinburgh. There is a heavy cloud of suspicion over his decision. Accusations were made that he had been poisoned. The theory that Mary promised a resumption of normal marital relations, if he agreed to be taken away from Glasgow, is decidedly shaky.

By the end of January he had been transferred to Kirk o' Field, an old house just inside the city wall of Edinburgh and less than a mile from Holyrood. Why Kirk o' Field? It was in a poor state of repair; it had not been regularly occupied; and, to make it habitable, furnishings and fuel had to be brought from Holyrood.

The room beneath that in which Darnley slept was

reserved for the Queen. But on the night that Kirk o' Field was blown up and Darnley with it, she was in Holyrood.

Mary had been openly associating with the Earl of Bothwell, a coarse, buccaneering figure, who was even more ruthlessly ambitious than Darnley. The blame for the explosion was immediately directed at Bothwell and a clique of noblemen.

Had the Queen been plotting her husband's death while she was in Glasgow? In later years, a bundle of papers which proved her downfall, the Casket Letters, contained a letter (or possibly more than one because the contents amounted to more than 2000 words) to Bothwell, apparently written in Glasgow that January. The Casket Letters have been said to be forgeries; if they were, they were composed with prodigious cunning. In the one to Bothwell from Glasgow, in which there are accounts of conversations between her and Darnley, it is stated: ' We are tied to two false races; the goodyere untie us from them.'

Bothwell was married. Mary, by the written description of two foreign observers of the time, was in an advanced state of pregnancy in the summer of 1567; the child could not have been Darnley's. The Queen's urgency in moving the sick Darnley from Glasgow to Kirk o' Field reinforces suspicions. He was not dying, and to murder him in Glasgow would have opened up much more dangerous consequences there and then.

The public accusations which were shouted through the streets on the day after the murder did not abate. On May 15, Bothwell, less than two weeks after divorcing his wife, was married to Mary in Holyrood, an exceedingly quiet wedding for a royal occasion. Many factors acted against the Queen; the jealousy and hatred of aristocrats, the distrust of the reformers, and now the violent opposition of many people, directed not simply at her but at her new husband. A month or so after the marriage, she was compelled to abdicate in favour of a Regent, the Earl of Moray. Imprisoned in Loch Leven Castle, she escaped the following year and found herself at the head of an army of supporters.

Mary had witnessed a few skirmishes and battles. A tall, tough woman, whatever her courtly wit and personal charms, she had once said she regretted not being a man so that she could campaign as a soldier. The battle she watched at Langside perhaps changed her mind on that and many other things.

Langside was then a hamlet on the side of a hill about two miles from Glasgow. Regent Moray, who had rejected a message from Mary, seeking to avoid a battle and possibly a civil war, had fortified the cottages there and had positioned his forces cleverly.

Mary was on horseback on a hill about half a mile away. Her troops, reportedly numbering about 6000, began to advance towards Moray but were badly hit by artillery, hidden in the gardens of the cottages. As they tried to press on uphill to gain hand-to-hand combat they suffered more

casualties. The battle lasted less than an hour. One account of it states that the Regent's army lost only one man while the Queen's army left 300 dead before it quit.

Without waiting for any kind of reckoning, Mary rode southwards with only a few companions. It has been said their fear was so great that they rode 60 miles to the Abbey of Dundrennan without halting.

Throwing herself on the mercy of her cousin, Elizabeth of England, she was given refuge. After being used as a political pawn for nearly ten years, she was executed. Bothwell, whom she disowned as a husband before she died, met his end in a Danish prison.

Glasgow had tried to stay clear of trouble. As happened so often in its history, it doggedly stuck to its own business, except to show just a margin of favour to what looked like the stronger side in the conflict around it. The city had a felicitous sense of placing its insurance.

Immediately after the battle of Langside, the bakers and victuallers reminded the Regent pointedly that they had supplied provisions for his army. At their suggestion, he expressed his thanks by granting permission to build a mill on the River Kelvin at Partick. Before that, they had been obliged to use grinding machinery on the lands of gentlemen farmers, who had imposed heavy charges on them. Flour is produced in mills there to this day.

The upheavals of the Reformation and the abortive revolt of the Queen's supporters had damaged the city's growth. There was need for stability and rehabilitation. The university had almost collapsed. (One account stated that the staff and students had dwindled to less than a score and the annual revenue to £25 English.) The value of the pound Scots, as against English money, was shrinking steadily, and trade was desperately poor.

The city's powers of adaptability came through strongly. Repairs to the Cathedral, damaged by the Reformation mobs, were financed from voluntary subscriptions and from taxes, levied by the town council. The council were not only very firm about the preservation of law and order, but also about the fixing of prices, fees, and wages. In a period of prolonged inflation towards the end of the 16th century, they were ruthless. Administration and law-making had developed a tough, Calvinistic fist of authority.

Andrew Melville, one of the greatest of the Reformers, had become Principal of the University in 1574 and within six years had achieved what seems an amazing upgrading of its fortunes and its academic standing. The supremacy of ecclesiastical power had passed away to be replaced by the Protestant pattern—more churches, more schools.

A system of rates for the relief of the poor was introduced in the city. The magistrates at the same time had ways of stopping any waste of money. For example, limitations were placed on the numbers invited to weddings for which, according to the bye-laws, the total sum spent should not exceed 1s 6d a head. An interesting Calvinistic note was the prohibition on holding Christmas

Day. The taking of salmon from the Clyde on Sundays was forbidden.

Being a magistrate was not a simple task of issuing a spate of bye-laws; they had to enforce them. A cordiner, called Thomas Craig, interfered with this when he stole the gallows one night and moved them to another place. They normally were positioned in the famous Gallowgate, an eastward route from the city centre. Hanging in those days was for thieves and lesser criminals. Prior to the middle of the 17th century murderers were beheaded.

Glasgow was still inside a wall, literally. There were ports and accesses, but only a few roads. Other settlements began to take a more definite shape around it. There were buildings on the lands of Gorbals across the river. In Govan, further downstream and on the same southern bank, there now lived people who farmed and fished and brewed ale.

In an unusual act of mutual co-operation, Glasgow and Dumbarton, commercial rivals, had cleared away a ford at Dumbuck to allow the passage of bigger ships. They were scarcely more than boats. It has been estimated that there were six or more, the largest being about 92 tons; and, because there was no harbour in Glasgow itself, they were moored in the middle of the shallow Clyde.

Lowland Scots business men and craftsmen dominated the life of the city. Not only had much of the ecclesiastical power structure been dismissed but the proportion of West Highland people had diminished. A list of burgesses of the early 17th century shows very few 'Macs', only six among 576 names.

In spite of Presbyterian supremacy in the area, there was still an Archbishop. The episcopacy had been retained by Act of Parliament in 1606. But the city had been determined to gain the freedom to elect its own magistrates, instead of simply accepting the nominees approved by the Archbishop. There was a good deal of quarrelling between the merchants and the craftsmen and at one time there was even rioting. In the end, the old electoral system was preserved.

The days of the episcopate were numbered, however. The movement for civic independence grew in the 17th century. It was honoured but not necessarily mollified by James VI (James I of Great Britain and Ireland), who granted the city a charter as a royal burgh. Glasgow never had much reason to thank the Stuart monarchs.

The Hammer of the Stuarts, Oliver Cromwell, entered the city in October, 1650. Scotland was in a sorry condition. The running battles of the royalists, the Covenanters, and the Ironsides had disrupted life in many parts of the country. Food stocks had been burned, towns impoverished, and now there was a situation close to famine.

Cromwell had pleaded with the Covenanters, who had started their divine crusade to immortalise God's chosen presbyterianism in Scotland and then decided to force it on England and Ireland as well. In one of his most famous statements, he thundered: 'It is therefore infallibly agreeable to the Word of God, all that you say. I beseech you in the bowels of Christ—think it possible you may be mistaken.'

He had given them cause to think again by defeating them at Dunbar. Now he was in Glasgow and he was probably not surprised that none of the civic leaders turned out to meet him because there had been many supporters of the Covenant in the city. The magistrates and others, in fact, had fled.

The Protector commandeered Silvercraigs House in the heart of the city. On the following Sunday he marched with his lieutenants to the Cathedral where a service was conducted in the lower Cathedral Church (place of worship of the Barony congregation) by the Rev. Zachary Boyd. Mr. Boyd took the opportunity to preach a biting, accusative sermon. Apparently undismayed, Cromwell asked him to dine at Silvercraigs House. After dinner and some theological discussion, the Protector invited Mr. Boyd to pray with him and then proceeded to pray for three hours. With his renowned salty humour, he had ways of bringing defiant clergymen to their knees.

Cromwell exhibited signs of generosity. He gave the university £200 which had been promised by the deposed Charles I and topped that with £500 of his own. But he does not seem to have been generally well disposed towards Glasgow and when fire ravaged about one-third of its houses two years later he commented that this could show 'the hand of an angry God'.

By the end of the century it had sustained even more damaging blows. One of Cromwell's soldiers had described it as not so big or rich and yet 'a much sweeter and more delightful place than Edinburgh'. In fact, it became bigger but decidedly poorer, and for a time it had reason to doubt its own enterprise and instincts for survival.

The restoration of the Stuart monarchy in Britain was considered by some Glaswegians to be an action comparable with deliberate importation of the plague. Parliament's approval of the English Navigation Acts excluded its traders from many of the colonies, the strengthening of the episcopacy against the supporters of the Covenant led to persecution and bloodshed in the city streets; and for every presbyterian martyr there were a dozen others, often the ablest and most enterprising, who went into voluntary exile.

The men who stayed and held the city together at that time were no angels. They were councillors and men of property, not always free of corruption. Their city had been punished by heavy fines, the population had declined, and hundreds of houses were uninhabited. For long periods it had been like an armed camp. There had been Scots and English troops, Danish mercenaries, and worst of all, a garrison of rapacious Highlanders. Indeed, there had been the passage of so many hungry armies that the town council had employed their own quartermaster at £10 a year to supervise food stocks and billeting arrangements.

John Anderson of Dowhill came to the forefront when creeds and causes, dogmas and divisions were destroying the basic fabric of living. For him, the city was a cause. 17

His family had spent their own money in raising arms to defend it.

When the Archbishop of Glasgow, John Paterson, fell foul of the Covenanters and was imprisoned in Edinburgh, Anderson struck a blow for independence. Representing the town council, he travelled to Hampton Court, London, to petition King William to grant the city freedom, as a royal burgh, to elect its own magistrates and councillors. He was successful and for his trouble he was created Provost and given £3673 for payment of expenses during his 145 days in London. The sovereignty of the archbishop, which had sometimes been exercised in preference of the landowners and against the interests of the working and trading people, had finally been abolished.

Freedom of elections (strictly from within the ranks of the burgesses, of course) could not of itself produce all the dynamism that was needed to restore the fortunes of the city. But the job was tackled with thoroughness. There was re-building to be carried out and strong demands for a revival of the shipping trade. The ruling elite were a tight little circle. They worked hard and expected the same of others. Magistrates cracked down on the workshy, the intemperate, and the itinerant (outsiders were asked to furnish a certificate of good character from their last residence before they could set up house in Glasgow). The merchants were mad for money.

John Anderson was prepared to negotiate a deal with an ugly, unpleasant individual—Tobias Smollett, father of the famous novelist. Smollett was Provost of Dumbarton, still a trading rival to Glasgow. Anderson negotiated an extremely advantageous pact under which tolls, harbour dues and other charges were abolished. Dumbarton retained control of one quay and received a few minor concessions. But Glasgow, although it was scarcely worthy of being called a port, gained something highly significant—direct, untrammelled access to the sea.

Its merchants had long since tried to escape the Dumbarton strictures by joining in a scheme to found a pier and a dock on the opposite side of the Clyde, on the south bank about 16 miles west of Glasgow. They called it Port Glasgow.

Anderson probably was delighted with his diplomatic coup. He was a thrustful man who liked to go straight to the heart of a problem and get it resolved quickly. He was also an indefatigable lobbyist, always ready to accost the influential with ideas for his businesses, his city, or his river.

At that time, although he did not know it, one of his great mistakes was about to catch up with him. It was the Darien Expedition. The results of it almost wiped out Glasgow's coffers and its confidence.

Enthusiasm for Darien had caught on like a tropical fever. City merchants had suffered bad times. Resentful at being debarred from most of the colonies, they had been searching for new, lucrative ventures like those which had paid off for their rivals in England. They were sending up good, presbyterian prayers for their own Eldorado.

A group called 'The Company of Scotland' was established by Act of the Scottish Parliament in 1695 to colonise Darien on the Isthmus of Panama. The English navigational and trading laws did not apply there. Prospectuses that held out the promise of timber, minerals, crops and other pickings turned the heads of a surprising number of canny Scots.

The founding company was of dubious origin and few people knew anything about living conditions in Darien.

Shares to the value of £400,000 were subscribed from many parts of Britain and abroad. Private subscriptions in Glasgow were estimated to be at least £56,000. The town council took an additional £3000 worth. By the standards of their budget at the time, it was an enormous sum. Even the university, on the personal advice of the principal, decided to risk £1000. There was a fever.

Anderson, whose own stake amounted to £1000, was enthusiastically hustling up and down the corridors of power trying to persuade the main sponsors that the whole expedition should sail from the Clyde. He was the arch apostle of the area but not totally selfless; he claimed £90 in expenses from the town council for his touting, which, as it turned out, had been unsuccessful.

The Darien Expedition began on July 25, 1698, when five ships sailed from Leith, near Edinburgh, with bags of seeds, roots, collections of agricultural implements and about 1200 people. They were supplemented by others who sailed later.

An estimated 2700 went to Darien and only about 40 ever returned. A combination of the effects of the climate, disease, and the hostility of the Spanish settlers there destroyed them.

English and Dutch subscriptions had been withdrawn before the first ships had departed. The major share of the loss was borne by Scotland.

Towards the end of December 1700, when John Anderson was feeling pleased with himself about the benefits he had won for Glasgow in his pact with Dumbarton, a ship limped into Greenock. It was called, ironically, the 'Speedy Return', and aboard it were the survivors of Darien. Until its arrival, no one had known of the total failure of the expedition. When the news reached Glasgow, some merchants, according to a contemporary record, were almost driven to suicide.

The effect was shattering. The city's pride as well as its purse had been punished. The collapse of confidence in business was intensified by the economic crises which gripped the whole of Scotland a few years later.

A great deal of rancour was directed at the town council, who were suspected of playing down corruption, and at the English. The proposals for the Union of the Parliaments of Scotland and England were opposed in Glasgow to the extent of rioting. Craft guilds and presbyterian ministers had a hand in fomenting it. Troops had to be despatched from Edinburgh to suppress it.

Few people seemed to foresee the enormous advantages Glasgow would gain from the Union. But after it was formed in 1707 the manufacturers and traders and ship-masters came streaming out of the Broomielaw like the new, moralistic, frugal Phoenicians of the western world.

For a start, the city recovered about two-thirds of the investments in the Company of Scotland through a settlement drawn up at the time of the Act of Union, which wound up the Company.

The Union allowed Glasgow's merchants to gain access to the American colonies. Sugar refining, soap making, and the production of linen and cotton cloths had already been established in the area. There was a range of potential exports that was quickly and success-fully developed.

The adaptability and the acumen in marketing that were shown brought the city more national and international recognition than it had ever known.

Ships sailed to Virginia and the Carolinas from Port Glasgow, Greenock, Irvine, and from ports in north-west England. They carried the growing volume of goods produced in the area. At times, there were simply not enough of them for charter. In 1716, the first vessel to be designed specially for the Virginia trade was built at Crawfordsdyke, Greenock.

Although some small vessels had been built before then for fishing and trading, that event probably constitutes the foundation of the great tradition of shipbuilding on the Clyde.

The harbour at Port Glasgow had to be enlarged. New docks were constructed at Glasgow's Broomielaw. The pace of expansion was prodigious. If a new scheme for profitable manufacturing was seen, it was promptly financed. If a new or improved technique was reported from another country, it was imported and copied. Skilled workers in the making of white linen were brought from Ireland and Holland. Glass blowers and bottle makers were hired from Spain.

To some of the older residents of the city, who had lived through the revolutionary turmoil of the late 1600s and the acute poverty of the early 1700s, it must have been a bewildering place. In the flood of prosperity during the 1720s, suburban houses were springing up in the old districts of Gorbals and Calton and the newly created village of Anderston. People were building shops, taverns, and even clubs.

Glasgow was a neat, relatively clean city. It was a much healthier place than Edinburgh, where citizens were still in the habit of throwing household waste from the windows of upper storeys on to the streets. The Glasgow magis-trates, by dint of fining offenders five merks, had almost stamped out that practice.

Street lights, a civic status symbol in those days, had been introduced in 1718. They were tallow wicks, mounted inside a cone of glass.

The bulk of the population lived closely together in the centre of the city between the High Street and the lower end of the Saltmarket, on the north bank of the Clyde. They lived in cottages or in tenement buildings. Although

some of the newly rich were starting to move out to rural villas, most of the prosperous merchants and craftsmen lived in flats near to their place of business.

Old wine was going into new bottles. In the more literal sense, too, there was a growing appetite for French and Spanish vintages, some of which were being smuggled into the country. There were traders who had little taste for the activities of the new, all-British Customs and Excise.

Although many of the wives and daughters of the merchants still made and bleached their own linen cloth at home, they were beginning to sample an exciting variety of imported fabrics and fashions in which they could afford to indulge. There were also the famous 'Glasgow plaids', highly commended by the Princess of Wales in London and fast becoming internationally known.

Along with the more mundane imports came the foibles, luxuries, refinements and snobberies of Western European civilisation. The city even boasted of a genuine French dancing master. The magistrates warned him against encouraging 'too great familiarity' between males and females. They insisted that the sexes receive their tuition in separate halls at his academy.

It was a hard-working city. Everyone from the fishermen to the nabobs of commerce commenced the day's labours before six or seven o'clock in the morning. Lunch was taken at 10 a.m. or shortly afterwards and tea, or some form of evening meal, between four and five p.m. Apparently not many of the business and professional men bothered to eat at home in the early evening. They dined in taverns or clubs and took themselves off to bed about nine p.m.

Cargoes of many kinds were shipped to America but the main factor in the city's success was the way in which it set the pace in the tobacco trade. A few of its boldest men outstripped the rest of Europe, not simply by capital-ising on the natural advantages that the Clyde offered —its sailing ships could reach Virginia in one week or two weeks less time than those from London or north-west England—but because of their skill in manipulating the trade.

The method in the early days was exchange or barter. A 'store system' was instituted by the Glasgow merchants on the American seaboard. Plantation owners and tobacco processors could consign their wares to depots and there exchange them for imported goods without waiting to sell the tobacco to specific customers in Britain. If there was any financial risk, it lay with the merchants, who had to find money to develop the warehousing network; but they took that risk gladly and swept up enormous dividends. It led to the promotion of an adventurous but strong banking system in the west of Scotland.

English merchants complained to Parliament about the success of the Scots in the colonies, alleging that their trade was based on defrauding the Customs and Excise. After a formal inquiry, the Lords of the Treasury rejected the complaint as groundless, arising from 'a spirit of envy'. That was in 1721. A few years later Glasgow's trade with the American colonies had doubled.

The merchants possibly had been exonerated of charges that they were cheating the king's revenue, but there was no doubt of the unpopularity of customs duties. A duty of three pence on each barrel of beer caused extensive rioting in 1725. Daniel Campbell, M.P. had voted in favour of it in Parliament. A mob attacked and destroyed his home, Shawfield House, which stood near the Clyde at the end of what is now Glassford Street.

When soldiers were sent to quell them the following day they stoned the soldiers, who then opened fire. In the fighting, nine people were killed and seventeen wounded. The Provost of Glasgow and the magistrates were incarcerated in Edinburgh Castle for allegedly supporting the rioters. After their release, the city had to pay fines and reparations (including £6080 to Campbell, who seems to have used that to buy the whole of the large island of Islay). Ironically, it is recorded in an account of the period that the £10,000 that Glasgow had to find was raised largely through a special tax on ale and beer sold within its own boundaries.

The city was booming at a time when most of the rest of Scotland, particularly the agricultural areas, lay under an archaic feudal regime which was slow to absorb new techniques in farming, textile manufacture and building.

Daniel Defoe found that when he toured the country. He had been in Scotland before the Union as an agent of the English Government, some people said to avoid his creditors.

The author of 'Robinson Crusoe' held an admiration for the Scots. He had been born in London and in his several careers as soldier, trader, journalist, and spy he had seen the cruel as well as the comfortable side of life. Basically, he was a non-conformist and free thinker. When he returned to Scotland after the Union he described himself as 'an opponent of high-flyers and Jacobites'. He was also possibly the most perceptive economic pundit and journalist of his time.

This hook-nosed, ugly, energetic little man was in Scotland in 1708 and in 1712. In the mid-1720s he published an account of his tours of Britain, in which he went out of his way to commend Glasgow.

To him it was 'one of the cleanliest, most beautiful, and best-built cities in Great Britain'. Besides that, he carefully catalogued its enterprise and industry, sending 'nearly fifty sail of ships every year to Virginia, New England and other English colonies in America'.

All that Defoe admired—the practical following hard on the heels of the visionary—came to pass in Glasgow. By the mid-1730s it had shaken off much of the politically-biased constraint from the south. By the 1740s it had snapped up the huge tobacco contract for France and its commercial status was expanding like its merchant's waistlines. Politics, or at least national politics, were of little concern to it unless they cast an unwelcome shadow over its ledgers. Glasgow had the characteristics of a city state.

Merchants and tradesmen, although occasionally at odds with each other, lived by precise and jealously guarded codes of conduct, the import of which was to protect their own interests but also those of the city. This was particularly true of the trades. They were self-help agencies, protectionist groups, rate-fixers, educationalists, guardians of law and order, and patrons of the arts—all at the same time.

Between the trades class and the merchants no insuperable demarcation line was drawn. The merchants tended to command greater rank and prestige, as they had done even before the horizons of commerce were extended in the early 18th century. But a craftsman who could produce surpluses of finished wares could also sell them and thus become a merchant. If a man was a burgess and a craftsman, he could achieve his promotion in class by marrying a merchant's daughter (preferably one of the younger, the less easily disposable, ones). The gradations of upward progress were as carefully set as the movements of some of the decorous dances that were becoming fashionable.

In the town council, the merchants were in the majority, although it was a narrow one. Again the rules were carefully laid down, just as they were for the payment of wages or standards of apprenticeship or charges to be levied on the wares of non-Glasgow craftsmen, whose goods were imported from only a dozen miles away. The town council fixed prices and, totally irrespective of national government, imposed local subsidies when they wished.

In the savagely cold winter of 1740, for example, (the year that the Thames was frozen over for more than two months) the council decided to try to offset the effects of the high price of food on the poor. At the time when the price of meal rose rapidly, they enlisted the Merchants House, the Trades House, and the ruling bodies of the presbyterian churches to join them in purchasing £3000 worth, which was sold at cost price. The money was borrowed and the repayment of interest was largely borne by the town council. In fact, that arrangement has been claimed as the start of the municipal debt, which in modern times has increased to hundreds of millions.

Nobody who had access to a few pounds of credit worried about debt in those days. There was still a sound presbyterian preference for cash on the barrelhead but to many people a dependable vein of prosperity had been struck. Glasgow's bills of exchange bore the infallibility of Old Testament texts.

The place itself was a kind of Eden of the newly rich, in spite of its burgeoning tan works and sugar refineries. McUre, the city's most celebrated historian of the 18th century, wrote that it was 'surrounded with cornfields, kitchen and flower gardens, and beautiful orchards, abounding with fruit of all sorts, which by reason of the open and large streets send forth a pleasant and odoriferous smell'.

Apart from the stinking, unsightly tanworks, there were probably other environmental problems, such as the residue of the old cottages. Or, for that matter, the use of Glasgow Green, which lies by the river and to the east of the old city centre. It is recorded that many women bleached their clothes on it and also that some gentlemen played golf on it; but it is not recorded whether they were compatible.

Bonnie Prince Charlie took the Green for more serious business. Prince Charles Edward Stuart, seeking to re-possess the throne of Britain for the Stuarts, landed in Scotland and, supported by an army of Highlanders, marched swiftly south in 1745.

Glasgow was opposed to him. Irrespective of the validity of his claims or any continuing dislike of the English, a city that was ardently making money did not welcome the idea of hordes of scruffy Highlanders interfering with the production and sales of goods. The Prince was a threat, as he demonstrated by an imperious demand for £15,000 and whatever arms could be found.

Guns? The city had been more concerned with the development of gentility than armouries. Paintings were being purchased by the affluent for the first time. The Foulis brothers were printing elegant editions of the Latin and Greek classics. There was a newspaper, ' The Glasgow Courant ', which had appeared, died, and re-appeared with such tasteful advertisements as that of James Hodge, announcing the selling of ' burying crepes ready-made, and that his wife's niece, who lives with him dresses dead corpses at as cheap a rate as was formerly done by her aunt, having been educated by her and perfected at Edinburgh, from whence she is lately arrived and has all the newest and best fashions '.

Now Bonnie Prince Charlie and his tartan tatter-demalions were on the doorstep, suggesting that if they did not receive their ransom then, by implication, Mr. Hodge's wife's niece would be working round the clock.

The Provost was Andrew Cochrane, one of the boldest, most imaginative men of his age. He chose to be defiant, but adaptable.

Playing his hand deftly, he first made it plain that the city remained loyal to the sovereign and considered the intruders as ' pretended princes and rebels '. Then he stalled until the main strength of the Jacobites had veered eastwards to meet the challenge of the King's army, which they subsequently defeated at Prestonpans, near Edinburgh. Left to deal with Prince Charles's quarter-master and less immediate threat of armed force, the city did not pay £15,000 but fobbed him off with £5000 in cash and £500 in goods.

As the Prince marched south into England, Glasgow raised two battalions, each of 600 men, to fight him. When he retreated from Derby back into Scotland only a month or two later, both battalions, unfortunately, had been deployed to defend Edinburgh. Once again Glasgow was at the Pretender's mercy—and this time he arrived in person.

In spite of the setbacks to his cause, he still cut a rakish, elegant figure. The ' Chevalier ', on his way south, had captivated the ladies of Edinburgh. At the snap of his fingers, Holyrood Palace had become a blaze of social gaiety. He was 25, slim, charming, and hopelessly addicted to women and drink.

On his arrival in Glasgow during Christmas, 1745, he was a different man, certainly more melancholy. But he still flaunted his royal style. He is said to have dressed in silk tartan with crimson velvet breeches, and occasionally his elegant court coat was adorned with insignia of the Order of the Garter. He took over the mansion of Shaw-field, which had been rehabilitated after the riots of twenty years earlier. Twice a day he chose to dine at a window seat so that the citizens could obtain a glimpse of him.

The ladies of Glasgow were not susceptible to his charms. Provost Cochrane, who testified that no one had much time for the Prince, noted: ' Our very ladies had not the curiosity to go near him, and declined going to a ball held by his Chiefs.'

Glasgow Green, Charles decided would be the setting for a great review of his troops. They marched and counter-marched with drums beating, bagpipes playing, and colours flying. He took the salute while standing under a thorn tree. It must have been a fairly sad sight on a chill, wintry day; much of his army was bedraggled and badly shod.

From the city he demanded 12,000 linen shirts, 600 cloth coats, shoes, tartan hose, blue bonnets, and money. The goods were delivered. The Prince left with his army and a new mistress, Clementina Walkinshaw, aged 19, with whom he had been having what was described as a ' hectic romance '. Her father was the local Laird of Barrowfield, whose family were active Jacobites for many years.

The city had been saved from burning and sacking. At one point it had seemed that some of the Highlanders wanted to take revenge on it. But they were stopped by the intervention of Cameron of Lochiel, who had about 700 followers in the Prince's army. In honour of that action, bells in the city centre are still rung each time a lineal descendant of Lochiel pays a formal visit to Glasgow as Chief of the Clan Cameron.

Provost Cochrane celebrated the withdrawal of the Jacobites with a vigorous statement of good riddance in which he said that they had taken only one military recruit ' one drunken shoemaker, who must soon have fled his country for debt, if not for treason '. Cochrane and his brother-in-law, a Bailie of the town council, later went off to London, where, after a tough political battle, they persuaded Parliament to pay the city £10,000 compensation for what the Jacobites had requisitioned.

News of the Prince's defeat at Culloden in 1746 was greeted with festivities in the streets, the holding of a cake and wine banquet, the sending of a deputation to present the victorious but ruthless Duke of Cumberland with a gold box containing the freedom of the city—and the playing of bells.

Glasgow was a bedlam of bells. In the latter part of the 18th century it was impossible to walk through the centre on any day without hearing them. The steeple of the Tolbooth, a high tower still standing at Glasgow Cross, could offer a different tune each day. On Sunday, for example, there was the 'Easter Hymn', while a somewhat lighter air, 'The Last Time I Cam' O'er the Muir', was thought more appropriate for Friday.

Apart from the many church bells—all of which were once inspected by order of the town council to ensure they had not been damaged by 'unskilled ringing'— there were the mart bell, the skellat bell, and bells rung up and down the streets by self-important men, making public announcements of all kinds. The city had an official bellman. One or two of them were raffish characters, Dougal Graham wrote a history of the 1745 rebellion in epic doggerel, and George Gibson ('Bell Geordie') was renowned for looking down his hugely malformed nose at some of the official proclamations and then making witty, derisory comments on them.

Bells rang when the low-draught boats brought herring to the Broomielaw and the fattest fish were sent along to the River Bailie of the town council for inspection. The din at times must have been intense. Years later, an English visitor wrote of Glasgow:—'La bells—damn—sans merci.'

In the 18th century there was a verse about Scottish towns:

> 'Lithgow for wells,
> Glasgow for bells,
> Falkirk for beans and peas
> Embro for . . .'

What was said of Edinburgh was shocking but probably true then—and institutionally libellous now.

The great and lucrative rise in trading that Glasgow enjoyed was attributed by Provost Cochrane to the talents and initiative of four young men. They reputedly had less than £10,000 among them when they started. They were Alexander Speirs of Elderslie, John Glassford of Dougalston, James Ritchie of Busby, and William Cunninghame, who became laird of the great estate of Lainshaw, Ayrshire.

Fortunes were made in weeks, rather than decades. Cunninghame, for example, was a junior partner in a company at the beginning of the American War of Independence. They held the largest tobacco stock then in Britain (bought for three pence a lb) and the other partners wanted to sell. Cunninghame took it over as his personal property and, by the time he had sold the last of it, the price was 3s 6d a lb.

They helped to found banks, they built huge mansions, and fitted out their country estates in royal style. Glassford had a wall built around the entire 30 acres of gardens of his house, less than two miles from his city office. The rent of his office was £13 a year and while he was still in his forties the return on his 25 sailing ships, the fastest afloat, was reportedly more than £500,000 a year.

By no means all of the merchants made fortunes out of tobacco; indeed, the profits of some were distinctly modest. There were probably greater gains to be made in the exports of textiles, hardware, and metals; to say nothing of soap, spirits and some other products.

Iron making, which had started in the district before the 1745 uprising, had been followed by simple forms of machinery manufacture. Looms were brought from England and Holland, copied, and in certain instances improved by local adaptation. The demands of the textile industries were unceasing. New employment on a large scale was created in bleaching and dye-making.

The term 'mechanic' came to be used in a general way for a man employed in a workshop or 'manufactory'. His average wage seven shillings a week. Oatmeal, herring and potatoes, mainstays of the local diet, were very cheap and beef was fourpence to sevenpence a lb. Rents were dear, by comparison with other parts of Scotland; they were at least thirty shillings to £2 a year. But the period between 1745 and 1785 was generally considered to be one of growing prosperity for all.

Undoubtedly at the apex of a more broadly based society, however, remained the tobacco merchants. Although there was a great deal of interest and investment in new industries, their commerce was the main source of wealth. For example, cambric fabrics, protected by Government legislation, encouraged by local subsidies, were regarded as a lucrative export commodity; but the foreign sales of all of Scotland's cambrics in a decade amounted to less than one tenth of what Glasgow earned from tobacco imports in one year.

The merchants were called 'Virginia Dons'. They came to favour scarlet cloaks and tricorn hats. In the course of a generation or two many of them became fiercely haughty and socially elitist. They might have rough Scots accents, they might have gone in their younger days as 'super-cargo' (combined ship's master and salesman) to the primitive communities of Virginia or the Carolinas, they might have a presbyterian awareness of the difficulties of rich men in graduating to heaven—but they wanted respect for their money.

In a city where the streets were often awash with mud and working women wore their skirts hitched to the knee, the 'Dons' promenaded on the 'plainstanes', near the equestrian statue of King William at Glasgow Cross, the only properly laid stretch of paving that existed. They tended to speak only to each other or to their head clerks. For anyone of distinctly lower orders to address them or lift his hat to them was deemed an insult. There was a high incidence of inter-marriage between their families.

In the business community generally there were so many Reids, Browns, Smiths, Buchanans, Campbells and other lowland Scots surnames that 'tae names' (nicknames) were commonplace. Unlike the characters in Sir Walter Scott's novels, who were frequently burdened with Biblical Christian names, Glasgow men at that time had mundane Christian names and middle names were considered exhibitionist.

David Hume

Adam Smith

James Watt

There were 26 men of property called James Brown. The one who had his business in the Exchange, therefore, was 'Broker' Brown. His near neighbour, who made glass beads or globular weights for the testing of spirits, was known as 'Bubbly' Brown. As for Campbells, there were 'Black Mungo' Campbell, 'Business Sandy' Campbell, 'Dignity' Campbell and others of more obscure title. In fact, they had all been baptised John Campbell and they were all fairly closely related.

The names to conjure with were all known well beyond Scotland. In Glasgow and Edinburgh were some of the greatest men of the age. There were David Hume, philosopher; his best friend, Adam Smith, author of 'The Wealth of Nations' and progenitor of the science of economics; James Watt, inventor of the separate condenser for the steam engine; Joseph Black, discoverer of latent heat; William and John Hunter, the famous physicians; and Robert Adam and his three brothers, the premier architects and designers of their time.

Adam Smith, a Kirkcaldy man, took up the appointment of Professor of Logic at Glasgow University and later became Professor of Moral Philosophy. He was a fervent clubman and social lion. Mixing with the Glasgow merchants and manufacturers, he had considerable influence over many of them and, in turn, learned much from them. Smith was a catalyst who precipitated a new ferment of ideas about the relative values of land, goods, and labour—and the best ways of maximising them.

In Glasgow University, he was revered. Students were sent to him from as far away as Moscow. Busts of him were placed in shop windows during his lifetime. Although scarcely handsome, he was an elegant figure. He did not prowl about the stage of the auditorium, like other professors, while delivering his lectures. Instead, he preferred to stand by a desk in a somewhat contrived pose and expound in a crisp, occasionally harsh tone. Admirers tended to copy his stammering English accented voice (he had studied at Oxford).

During his addresses to clubs and business associations in Glasgow, he stimulated interest among an extraordinary assortment of people. Little of the great talk or the dialogues has been recorded. Smith, in any case, frowned on anyone taking notes while he was speaking; he liked to protect his ideas and detested 'scribblers'.

In a series of lectures outside the university, he identified 'the natural price of commodities' and 'the natural price of labour'. Much of the material he used in them, plus the essence of others, entitled 'Justice and Policy', (delivered to his moral philosophy class) seem to constitute the groundwork of 'The Wealth of Nations', published long afterwards.

Once, while showing a young politician round a hide works, he became so animated in offering his theories about labour costs that he fell off the plank on which they were standing and landed in the sludge of the tanning pit. He was pulled out, cleaned, and sent home in a sedan chair.

Probably on his undignified return journey that day he was in no mood to ruminate about new factors in the economic system. But if he had looked around him he might have detected the first tentative assertions and alliances that betokened the foundation of the trade union and co-operative movement.

Sedan chairmen, for example, wanted to form their own association. The increasing number of tobacco spinners or processers had the same aspirations. They were not trades in the old-established sense but eventually (in the 1770s) their wishes were granted. The town council accorded them seals of cause as minor incorporations.

By then, there was already a trade union, the society of porters or workmen, authorised by the town council to levy money for their elderly or sick members. Each porter was given a badge. Porters or others who were not members were liable to a fine of five shillings if caught doing a porter's job. The horse setters and hirers quickly followed suit by forming their own association.

The town council's powers were boundless. They exercised direct control over most of the growing industries and where the rules of the merchants or the guilds did not apply they instituted new rules. For example, in the making of stockings they dictated that there should be a fine imposed for every imperfect pair that was sold and that every pair which passed inspection must bear the stamp 'Glasgow'.

In the latter part of the 18th century, as the exercise of their authority became more and more complex, they were very conscious of the dangers of unrest among the workers in the mills and factories.

They were building new roads as well as the new bridges that straddled the Clyde and the Kelvin. For some reason, possibly pressure from city traders, they chose to finance bridges in various parts of southern Scotland. They subscribed for one at Coldstream, near the English border. Money was borrowed copiously even recklessly, and big schemes of public works were encouraged.

The grand design, of course, was the eventual deepening of the Clyde to allow the passage of large ships all the way from Glasgow to the sea.

Confidence, drive, a sense of achievement—Glasgow was rife with them; bustling and bell-ringing like a madhouse of tills. In the change-houses, the mansions, and the taverns the greatest expectations were not questioned and the wonders of the age seemed to change with the frequency with which gentlemen now changed their shirts. The magistrates had voted themselves heavily symbolic gold chains of office but enterprise was unchained and unchallengeable.

Two or three schemes for deepening the Clyde had been discarded before the town council asked the famous engineer, John Golborne of Chester, to make a survey in 1768. He reported that it was 'extremely practicable'. But they did not proceed until they had received a second report, this time from a man who later became known as one of the world's greatest engineers—James Watt of Greenock.

Watt had already laid out the master plan for the Forth and Clyde Canal (built between 1768 and 1790) across central Scotland. He had also designed Scotland's first graving dock at Port Glasgow.

When Watt corroborated Golborne's ideas, permission was obtained from Parliament to begin gouging out the Clyde. Considering the kind of earth-moving equipment and pier-forming techniques available at that time, the work appears to have been carried out at an extraordinary pace in the early 1770s. Golborne supervised it, assisted by his nephew. Their annual salary: £220.

A channel nearly eight feet deep was cleared from the Broomielaw to Dumbuck. The town council, the Trades House, and the Merchants House were so pleased that Golborne was commissioned to extend it. They were even moved to give him a special gratuity of £1500.

The whole enterprise, including compensation paid to one of the local landlords and to the towns of Renfrew and Paisley, probably cost less than £25,000. It was the beginning of a prodigious feat of engineering which altered the course of the city's history. Other great engineers, notably Telfer and Rennie, later contributed to the completion of this famous waterway. If it had not been created, Glasgow today might have been a modest cathedral city by a river, like Worcester on the Severn.

James Watt was one of the few local men of international renown who had an effect on the destiny of the city and its people. The school primer type of popular image of him—the planner of harbours and waterways, and, of course, the man who envisaged a revolutionary steam engine while walking alone on Glasgow Green—does not do justice to the incredible range of innovations he brought to the greater good of Glasgow and of Scotland.

In his lifetime there was a golden age. Incidental lustre was added to it by the historical figures who visited the city.

In the village of Gorbals across the river there were green fields and thatched cottages. Many of the cottages were destroyed one summer night by a widespread fire. The city by then had its own fire brigade, but they were happy to receive the help of a party of soldiers, led by a young officer. He was Major James Wolfe, later to become General Wolfe who stormed the Heights of Abraham to defeat the French in Canada.

During his term of service in Glasgow he stayed in Camlachie House. Military duties seemed to be scarcely demanding. He undertook the social whirl with gusto, regularly being invited to the homes of the rich. To maintain his appetite for culture (he said in a famous remark later that he would rather have written Gray's 'Elegy in a Country Churchyard' than have taken Quebec) he engaged a tutor for two hours a day to foster his Latin and other studies.

In the social bagatelle, every base he touched he illuminated. He was acclaimed for being exceedingly polite and charming. Naturally, he was popular with the ladies. They never suspected what he had written to a friend. Glasgow women, he had observed, were 'coarse, cold and cunning'.

The 'Elegy', which Wolfe admired, might have been published in Glasgow. Thomas Gray, that strange little man with piercing eyes and bright, pink cheeks, came north to meet the Foulis brothers just after Dodsley of London had begun publishing his work. He arranged for a book of poems under their imprint. In fact, he judged their printing to be so superior that he wished that they had been his publishers from the first.

He may have said that, of course, simply to please the local literati who at that time were blooming in the fullest, provincial purple. They convened literary breakfasts. They doted on the old classics and some of the new philosophers. In the Anderston Club on Saturdays they applauded Professor Simson's recitals of Greek verse.

When the formidable Dr. Samuel Johnson came in 1773, accompanied by James Boswell, his biographer, he sat down to a literary breakfast with three professors in the Saracen's Head Inn. He was not amused; they were not intellectually stimulating enough for his taste. When the Foulis brothers dropped in, he found them even less pleasing.

Boswell, who had been a student at Glasgow University and later had been fortunate to have his early works published by the brothers, noted in his 'Journal of a Tour to the Hebrides with Samuel Johnson, LL.D.' that the doctor had found them tiresome conversationalists. 'Instead of listening to the dictates of the sage, they had teased him with questions and doubtful disputations.' By then, of course, Boswell was well settled into his role of manager and publicist of the heavyweight champion of British letters.

Did Johnson have a short, angry encounter with the great Adam Smith? It has been passed down through literary folklore that he did. The two men had met before in London when Smith, who had been extolling the virtues of Glasgow, was on the receiving end of one of Johnson's celebrated snubs.

When they met in Glasgow in 1773, it is said, they snarled at each other, Johnson called Smith a liar; and, in reply, Smith called Johnson something much worse. Long afterwards, Sir Walter Scott, who occasionally stayed at the Saracen's Head and may have had proof of the encounter, accused Boswell of deliberately omitting it from his 'Journal'.

At any rate, Johnson was well pleased by the cuisine and comforts of that Gallowgate inn. According to some accounts, it was erected on an old burial ground with stones taken either from the ruins of the Bishop's Palace or from the Gallowgate Port, one of the city gates demolished in the 1750s. For 150 years—it was demolished in 1905—it was Glasgow's most famous inn, visited by many famous people such as Thomas Gray, Robert Burns, and William Wordsworth.

Burns came to Glasgow during a grave emotional 27

crisis in his life. It was early in 1768 and he was planning to emigrate to Jamaica with one of the current loves of his life, Mary Campbell, 'Highland Mary', who was to die tragically at Greenock several months later.

The story goes that he travelled to the city with his poems, as yet unpublished, and a letter of introduction to one of the staff of Dunlop & Wilson, the booksellers and printers in the Trongate. The young man to whom he showed his poems was impressed. He said enthusiastically: 'Don't talk of the West Indies, sir—Edinburgh, not Jamaica, is the place for you.'

Dunlop & Wilson, however, would not publish them, and no other Glasgow printer was willing. Burns turned sadly back to Ayrshire. The story (which is possibly over-romanticised) adds that on the way he stopped off at the print shop of Wee Johnny Wilson, near the Market Place in Kilmarnock, and thus the famous 'Kilmarnock Edition' was born.

Eighteen months later, after he had been to Edinburgh and lavishly feted there as 'Caledonia's Bard', he was back in Glasgow. He had a small number of friends with whom he corresponded and through them he met the woman with whom he was to have the most delicate and restrained of his many love affairs—Mrs. Agnes MacLehose. Her husband had abandoned her and gone to Jamaica.

Mrs. MacLehose was the well-bred daughter of a Glasgow surgeon. The society in which she moved was that of the 'Virginia Dons' and the clerics. A different genre from the country girls that Burns had chased from hayrick to penitent stool, she brought out possibly the best in him as a gentleman and the worst as a poet.

In their letters and his verses, she was 'Clarinda' and he was 'Sylvander'. He stayed at the Black Bull Inn at the end of Virginia Street, he visited her, and he wrote profusely. In February 1788, at the peak of their corres-pondence, there were four letters in two days. Their friendship lasted for four years. They parted memorably in Edinburgh in 1791. Mrs. MacLehose went to the West Indies but returned in 1793.

Burns once described a Glasgow merchant as a 'plunderer of armies'. Richard Oswald possibly deserved that title. He allegedly built up a fortune as Chief Com-missary of Supplies to the British Army. Son of a poor Caithness minister, he married a rich heiress and gained control of large plantations in America and the West Indies.

Glasgow honoured Oswald for his services to the city. These were political services. He lived mostly in London, where he wielded considerable influence among Members of Parliament and the Government.

The victories of the American colonists in the War of Independence were like fiercely struck nails in the coffin of the tobacco merchants. They had helped to raise the Glasgow Regiment of 900 men (no English recruits were admitted) to fight in America. Every man was made a free burgess and given a generous bounty. It was an elegantly dressed but pathetic little army which ended as the figurative funeral escort for the 'Virginia Dons'.

Strangely, it was Oswald who played a key part in the termination of the war. He had been introduced to one of the Government's principal ministers by Adam Smith. The Government did not want to be seen suing openly for peace with the Americans. Oswald, who had many business associates there, was asked to conduct negotia-tions in secret. He travelled to Paris to meet the com-missioners of the new United States and arranged the terms of the peace treaty which was subsequently signed in 1783.

At the peak of the expansion of the tobacco trade Glasgow merchants had purchased entire crops in advance of planting or they had bought outright the plantations themselves. Many of these plantations were now con-fiscated by the independent states of America. As they developed their own commercial avenues for export, they tended largely to by-pass Glasgow as a port of entry.

Several of the eminent merchant houses of the city dwindled into insignificance even before the termination of the war. James Buchanan, who had been Lord Provost of Glasgow was made an inspector of the police at £100 a year but the town council had to take steps to prevent any of his creditors arresting his salary. He had lost nearly everything. Another member of the same family, Andrew Buchanan, planner of one of the city's main shopping thoroughfares, died in poverty in 1784.

Traders and agents, who had lived in America and had invested their profits in estates in Scotland, tried to raise tobacco at home. In the main, they were prosperous men who had taken themselves off to early retirement in the rolling, green hills of the Borders. A Dr. Jackson grew tobacco on a small scale near Kelso in 1781. When it was learned that he sold it allegedly for 2s 6d a lb, there was, in the words of a local man, Thomas Somerville, 'a rage of speculation'. Others, also from America, had grown it before then but not with such lucrative results.

In the spring of 1782 many hundreds of acres of arable ground between the Forth and the Tweed were planted. Unfortunately, that was a particularly severe winter and only about one-twentieth of the crop was fit for marketing.

Glasgow merchants, who still had imported stocks in their warehouses, protested to the Government. They, in turn, were totally confused about how to treat this strange, new agriculture. In the end, they decided it could not be exempted from payment of duty, they empowered the Commissioners of Customs and Excise to buy it at a fair price (around 4p a lb), and the crop was taken to Leith to be burned.

Glasgow in that dire winter of 1782 was a miserable city. The harvest had been a failure, immigrants from surrounding counties and from as far away as the West Highlands were pouring into the city—and to add to the hardship the Clyde came pouring into the city. Homes and warehouses were flooded as the river ascended to 20 feet above its normal level. Food and dry clothing were taken in boats to people in Gorbals and around the Saltmarket and Bridgegate.

As the shortage of foodstuffs had been worsened by the destruction of supplies in warehouses, the magistrates issued an appeal to all farmers in the region to bring their meal to Glasgow market, where they would be paid 6d a boll above the ordinary price.

Glasgow had to salvage its pride, too. Once again it needed to demonstrate its powers of adaptability. Looking outwards, there were some consolations. There were still strong commercial ties with the West Indies. An independent America could yet be attractive as an export market.

Looking inwards, Glasgow had to find the best means to develop local resources. In particular, it needed to utilise the multiplying ranks of available manpower. It was a time of social upheaval at every level. A new breed of leaders was beginning to replace the old merchant class. The city was still a fairly beautiful place, notably around Glasgow Green and on the western outskirts; but the growth of incoming population was starting to be troublesome. Problems of over-crowding, drunkenness, and lawlessness were suppurating.

Justifiable or not, a strong feeling existed that Glasgow had been neglected, indeed mistreated, by Parliament and the Governments of the previous two decades. Bungling in the mercantile and taxation laws, mishandling of foreign affairs (particularly the American war) and other accusations were commonly directed at Westminster.

In 1783, more than 200 merchants combined to form Glasgow Chamber of Commerce for the protection of its trade and industry. It was the first chamber of commerce in Britain.

The principal founder and author of its constitution was Patrick Colquhoun, Provost of the city and a brilliant social reformer. As a 16-year-old orphan he had gone to Virginia. After spending his early manhood in the tobacco trade, he returned to Scotland and participated in an assortment of businesses. He was a versatile, indefatigable man, who persuaded the Government of William Pitt to develop and encourage the cotton industry of Glasgow and Lancashire. Later he became a nationally recognised expert on social economics, crime control, education, and the relief of poverty.

One of the founders of the Chamber of Commerce was a man who exemplified the new breed of civic leaders and, in many ways, embodied the spirit of adaptability and enterprise that saved Glasgow. He was David Dale, then 43, a fat man with a couthy turn of phrase and a capacity to take a joke against himself.

Dale, a shopkeeper's son from Ayrshire who had worked his way up from weaver's apprentice and clerk to textile baron, had a pervasive Christian conscience. He was an unorthodox man, a lay preacher, who taught himself Hebrew and Greek to read the scriptures.

When he became a Glasgow magistrate it was the custom for the town council to go, usually once a year, to a presbyterian church for the 'kirkin' of the council'.

Burns

'Clarinda'

But he was head of his own breakaway church in the relatively new suburb of Anderston. Would he go to the usual service with all its stately procession and ceremonials? There was widespread interest and controversy in the city.

Dale struck out for the right to go his own way. As all the others solemnly paraded to church he walked through the streets to his own place of worship, the 'Caun'el (Candle) Kirk'—with an armed escort, just like the rest.

In the year that the Chamber of Commerce was founded, he not only became the first agent for the Royal Bank in Glasgow but he also persuaded the famous Sir Richard Arkwright, inventor of the 'spinning jenny', to go into partnership with him in establishing large mills for cotton spinning at New Lanark, south of Glasgow.

The mills still stand, a decaying monument to a great experiment in paternal socialism. Dale gave employment to more than 1300 people at a time. He provided houses for the workers. There were schools and nurseries for their children. When they came of suitable age (admittedly, very young by contemporary standards) the children were given employment in teasing and picking cotton by hand. He looked after immigrants from the Highlands and provided unheard of opportunities for orphaned and destitute children.

Dale made one or two mistakes in his wide-ranging career as the key figure in the development of the cotton industry in Scotland, but they were insignificant when compared with his triumphs. Abetted by different partners, he founded spinning mills in several parts of the west of Scotland; he reaped enormous profits and commissioned the illustrious Robert Adam to build a fine house for him in Glasgow; he gave away large sums and personally imported shiploads of grain to feed the poor; and he brought to the new radicalism of the time a spiritual lustre, which, unfortunately, few others could sustain.

The winter in which Dale, Colquhoun and the rest came together to launch the Chamber of Commerce was one of appallingly cruel weather. There have been almost no winters in the twentieth century to match the disastrously extreme conditions experienced several times in the previous two or three centuries.

Flooding, caused by heavy rain, was familiar. The freezing of the Clyde was less common but it occurred to some degree every generation or two. Early in the 17th century, for example, there was the sad story of Ninian Anderson. He obtained from the town council a franchise for the Stockwell Bridge, which empowered him, on payment of a fee of £17 10s a year, to charge a toll on everyone who crossed between the old heart of the city and the lands of Gorbals. Unfortunately, that year the Clyde was frozen solid for about 15 weeks and few people bothered to use the bridge then. The town council were gracious enough to heed his complaints and allow Mr. Anderson a rebate of £3 6s 8d.

People who thought the winters of 1780 and 1782

extremely severe had worse to come in 1785. The Clyde was solidly frozen, according to some accounts of the period, for as as long four months. Reminiscent of the more famous scenes when the Thames in London was a temporary causeway of ice, Glaswegians built booths and held markets and carnivals on it.

That was the year in which a man called Neil McLean was hanged for forgery. The execution was conducted in the old yard of the Bishop's Palace. Several years later work began on the building of a hospital, the present Royal Infirmary, on the site of the former Palace. The designer was Robert Adam. Glasgow's first hospital had been founded in the latter half of the 15th century and at least two others were in existence before the Royal Infirmary was built.

Construction work on that meant that the gallows had to be moved yet again. They had an odd, unstable history. Once, when they were on their original site, in the Gallowgate, they had been stolen and moved to another place by a cordiner, who apparently had some complaint about the mechanics of law enforcement.

But a man who had no complaint about it was John McClelland, who was to be hanged, but on September 7, 1605, was offered a reprieve, if he took on the job of being city hangman. Apparently, the job was difficult to fill then. McClelland readily accepted, but he was so pestered and abused by an indignant public that the town council brought in an ordinance, imposing a fine of £5 Scots on anyone found bothering the city hangman.

Glasgow knew macabre and sensational murders long before Madeleine Smith; or Dr. Pritchard, the poisoner; or Peter Thomas Anthony Manuel, who killed seven, eight, or possibly nine people in the 1950s.

One of the most extraordinary was the killing of the town clerk, Robert Park, in his office in 1694 by Major James Menzies. The major, commanding a military garrison, had imprisoned several burgesses and Mr. Park had been trying to negotiate their release. In a quarrel, he was run through with a sword. The major ordered troops to facilitate his escape by blocking the streets. A rather illustrious posse, including a member of the Privy Council, the next provost, and several burgesses pursued him successfully, nevertheless. He was cornered and shot to death in Renfield Gardens, near to what is now the commercial centre of the city. An attempt was made, unsuccessfully, to prosecute and hang the ones who had caught him.

Of the two dozen executions conducted at the new site of the gallows at the Tolbooth, Glasgow Cross, in the years between 1788 and 1813, the one which aroused most public interest was that of James McKean, who was convicted of the murder of Andrew Buchanan, the Lanark carrier (horse-drawn wagon driver), by cutting his throat. McKean tried to escape on a sailing packet from Irvine to Ireland. It was pursued by a small brig and he was arrested on the island of Arran—reading the Bible.

The trial was truly sensational. On the morning of his execution at the Tolbooth, drizzling rain was falling and as the deputation of magistrates emerged to fulfil their legal role as witnesses of the hanging, McKean said: ' Dinna come oot, your honours, to weet yoursel's.'

His body was later given to anatomists for dissection. A small group of city merchants asked for skin off his back. The anatomists duly handed over specimens, tanned and cut into circles, and these were distributed as macabre souvenirs.

The case that led to judges stopping the practice of ordering the bodies of hanged criminals to be transferred to anatomists occurred about 20 years later. A welter of violent feeling had arisen against these doctors and physicians and, more particularly, against those who provided the corpses. Years before the celebrated Burke and Hare scandal in Edinburgh there had been riots in Glasgow, during which doctors' homes and part of the university medical school had been damaged. Bodies had been taken from local cemeteries and some had been found at the Broomielaw in sacks, imported from Ireland and consigned as meal or potatoes. The providers of corpses were ' resurrectionists ' but one case came too close to resurrection for the comfort of the judges.

The body of Matthew Clydesdale was taken from the gallows to be used in an experiment in galvanising, which was then in vogue among scientists. It was placed in a semi-upright position in a chair and tubes were inserted in the nostrils. Soon afterwards, the effects from electric battery charges began to be seen. It is recorded that the chest heaved, the lips began to move, the eyes opened, and eventually the body stood up and lurched forward. Students fainted.

Dr. James Jeffrey who was supervising the experiment, grabbed a scalpel and plunged it into Clydesdale's jugular vein. There is more than one account of this event. It is eminently possible, to judge from reports of other badly conducted hangings, that Clydesdale was not dead when taken from the gallows.

Crime was increasing almost inevitably at that time. Between 1791 and 1811 the population rose from 42,000 (64,000 if the suburbs of Gorbals, Calton, Grahamston and Anderston were included) to more than 110,000. For the poor of Ireland and of the Highlands of Scotland this city was the immigrants' best and most attainable refuge. There were jobs for them in the textile industries. Finding houses for them was becoming more difficult towards the end of the 1700s.

An element of the city's history long under-stated is that some of the first and most violent uprisings by organised groups of British workers were staged in Glasgow. Weavers, demanding legislation to fix basic wages, smashed mills and warehouses in Anderston in 1785. Two years later Glasgow heard again the crunch of army boots and the rattle of gunfire when the cotton workers of the Calton area· rioted. They were fighting against cuts in wages brought about by the influx of migrant workers, who were easily trained and were desperate for almost any kind of jobs.

The Riot Act, or its equivalent of the time, was read at Parkhouse. east of the cathedral. In a pitched battle in Duke Street between troops and strikers, several men were killed.

A small police force was started by the town council the following year. There was an inspector, a clerk, and eight men who dressed in scarlet uniforms with numbered badges. But they could scarcely cope with the roughnecks and petty thieves who were coming into the city. Festering under the surface and always likely to erupt into violence was another relatively new or enlarged problem—Protestant antipathy towards Roman Catholics, most of them Irish incomers.

In the large, suburban villas of the rich the social carousel was, if anything, more resplendent and exclusive than it had been in an earlier generation. The more douce and venerable of the merchants and manufacturers were perturbed about what they saw as the spreading radicalism of the French Revolution. But they probably told one another, in good Scots terminology, that they had ' never died a winter yet '.

The local economy, which revived with astonishing vigour after the collapse of the American tobacco trade, was banking the benefits of bigger and bigger imports of cotton, sugar, rum, coffee, timber and fruits from the West Indies. Heads of companies were backing industrialisation as if it was a sign, come down from a presbyterian Heaven. They recruited one or two English engineers here, a French chemist there; money was no object, they wanted the best—quickly. Thanks to James Watt, they were well versed in the advantages of machine power.

But the outbreak of war between the newly founded republic of France and Great Britain in 1793 dealt them a shattering blow. Immediately, a huge tract of the export market for textiles was closed to them. Imports of raw cotton from some sources were halted. Twenty-six banks collapsed that year. Three of them were Glasgow-based banks, only one of which eventually paid off all its creditors.

Not long after that, one of the greatest merchant houses that Scotland had ever known began to totter and finally it crashed spectacularly. It was that of Alexander Houston & Company, owners of enormous holdings in the West Indies. They had suffered in the general disturbance of trade, but one of the main reasons given for their downfall was unusual—they had been speculating in slaves.

Anticipating the endorsement by Parliament of a Bill for the emancipation of slaves, they had spent large sums to amass a supply of them before a legal deadline closed the market, The Bill, although introduced, was not approved. They were left with many unsold slaves whom they had to maintain but could not employ.

Glasgow, as an influential trading centre in the 18th century, did not approve of slavery. At least, most people did not approve and certainly did not care to see evidence of it in their own environs. The fact remains that some of its merchants were involved directly or indirectly in the slave trade.

After the failure of the Darien expedition, some of the dubious, marginal activities of the Company of Scotland were found to include slave trading on the east coast of Africa. At least two ships, financed in Glasgow, were used.

In 1708, a petition about trade, sent from the city to the new House of Commons in London, is understood to have contained a broad hint that Glasgow wanted the same access to the African slave trade as was granted to certain English enterprises. Glasgow Chamber of Commerce in the 1780s found slavery vexatious but refused to come out against it, and as late as 1833 they were still equivocal about it.

The spread of plantation ownership in the West Indies throughout the 18th century gave rise to bigger crop harvesting. There is evidence that Glasgow owners were responsible for the purchase of slaves, although the quantities are not known.

John Wedderburn was one buyer. He brought a black slave back to Glasgow. The man, Joseph Knight, was the originator of a strange and complex legal action in 1774. He had become a familiar sight, accompanying his master in the streets. But when Wedderburn wanted to send him abroad, he resisted, they quarrelled, and he petitioned for his liberty, alleging mistreatment.

A significant fact is that a group of ' Glasgow gentlemen' subscribed £500 towards the negro's legal expenses.

Local justices of the peace supported the master against the slave in the first phase of the case. But a Sheriff, to whom it was later referred, found that the law of Scotland did not recognise the state of slavery, and his ruling was upheld by the judges of the Court of Session. Knight walked out, a free man.

Nearly twenty years later, however, Glasgow men were still buying and selling slaves. One of the losers in the crash of the house of Houston was a partner in that company, James McDowall. He was Provost of Glasgow. Apparently, he was ignorant of the extent of the speculation in slaves.

The Provost was probably more familiar with a new type of man who was beginning to appear in the city—the speculative builder. New thoroughfares, flanked by taller buildings, began to change the central area. In the outer districts, there were the first good streets of terraces and tenements, which by the early 1800s set the character of some of them both socially and architecturally. They tended to be fairly long lines of cream-coloured or biscuit-coloured stone frontages, not yet affected by industrial grime. The new residential areas, even in the earliest stages, were noted for their spaciousness and solidity rather than any high style.

The protracted war against the French did not evoke vivid examples of patriotism at the start, although later the city was not stinting with its men and money. It was, to paraphrase an appropriate part of Dickens' writings, the best of times for some, the worst of times for a great

William Wordsworth

Dorothy Wordsworth

Kirkman Finlay

many. Agriculture in Scotland was in a state of disorder and inflation was rampant. Crops failed, the price of wheat almost doubled within five years, and in 1800 there were ' bread riots ' in Glasgow.

One person in every ten died of smallpox. The virulence of it, or at least its capacity to kill, seemed to have escalated. The town council set up a special committee to find out the value of the new wonder, a vaccine, developed by Dr. Edward Jenner in England. A few years later, in 1808, they were so grateful for his discovery that they broke away from their ' war effort ' in honouring a succession of generals and regiment founders to accord Jenner the freedom of the city.

The reverse was offered to those who did not respect the city's property. Proud of their new pavings and tidier streets, the town council cracked down on bonfires, noise, and the throwing of stones. Boys were not allowed to spin tops or to play shinty (a robust Highland hockey) on the pavings. Anyone who reported them for that received a reward of £5, if the boys were convicted.

But it was a fast-growing place, with one layer of workers' families being stacked above another layer in the older tenements, and children could not easily be stopped from playing in the streets. They played ' tig, tow, and touch wood ', ' smugglers and gaugers ', ' I spy ', ' Tumble the wulcat ' and ' roundabout, roundabout merry-matanzie '. Many of these games, played in the early 19th century, have lasted, in one form or another, well into the twentieth, especially the girls' skipping-rope games.

Older people sometimes indulged in rougher sports. Cock-fighting was well known in the east end of the city and in the Gorbals. In Govan every New Year's day card sharps, jugglers, tinkers and others liked to make a raucous fair of it when the ' shooting the cock ' sports were held. A cock was loosely tied to a stake. Apprentice tradesmen and young bloods in from the country would try to shoot it at a penny a shot. They usually fired an assortment of old guns, sometimes home-made guns. The marksman who shot each bird kept it.

A distaste for the coarser glimpses of Glasgow life quite spoiled the visit of William Wordsworth and his sister, Dorothy, in 1803. Naturally, they stayed at the Saracen's Head Inn, by then regarded by literateurs as a homely bothy on the remoter slopes of Parnassus. They arrived, with Samuel Coleridge, in an unusual private coach. Children chased after it, hooting as they went. Dorothy developed a headache.

The great punch bowl was still at the head of the table as it had been in Dr. Johnson's time. It had a capacity of several gallons. However, the dark golden days of ' Glasgow Punch ' were by then drawing to an end. It had been the favourite drink, by far exceeding Scotch whisky, which gained wide popularity in Glasgow only in the early part of the 19th century.

' Glasgow Punch ' consisted of West Indian rum, diluted with three to five parts of water usually, and flavoured with sugar plus the juice of limes or lemons.

The man of the house, by tradition, took off his jacket to mix it in a china bowl; the ceremonial was often accompanied by a mild speech of praise for the rum or a boast that he knew the very acreage of the tropics from which the limes had come.

The fruit was important. Mr. George Wardrop, who sold fruit in Bell's Wynd, offered a contract to customers to buy a year's supply of lemons in advance at a guaranteed price. He commended this as a wise precaution, adding in his droll advertisement: ' It is hoped this will prevent the gentlemen's drinking punch with cremitartar (cream of tartar) instead of lemons, which several has owned their being the worse of it.'

The Wordsworths did not feel themselves the better of the hospitality in the Saracen's Head. There were many noisy coaches in the area. The inn was the terminus of the London Mail. However, they were impressed by the vast Tontine Rooms at Glasgow Cross, the social centre for the elite. Dorothy Wordsworth called it: ' The largest coffee room I ever saw.'

In the Tontine, some of the city fathers talked about the peace with the French, recently broken, and how this man, Napoleon, could be vanquished. Resumption of the war seemed to provoke a flourish of patriotism. Regiments were raised by the Trades House, the grocers and others. A great parade was staged on Glasgow Green, where field guns and rifles were fired, generally for the benefit of recruiting and the entertainment of the hosts of spectators. It was a distant, not quite credible war, during which Glasgow continued to be more concerned with trading than with any idea worth all the bayonets of Europe. There were even stories that many of the boots, worn by the French troops in Egypt, had been made in King Street. A few merchants had been running contraband to Europe.

They rejoiced over Admiral Nelson's victory at Cape Trafalgar in 1805 and decided to raise a monument to him (badly damaged by lightning in 1810, but still standing on the Green). They mourned the death of one of their own sons, Sir John Moore, in a spectacular battle with the French at Corunna in Spain in 1809. Moore, a brilliant soldier who had campaigned in Corsica and the West Indies before the Peninsular War, was a descendant of Provost John Anderson of Dowhill, who had achieved so much for the independence of Glasgow.

In the city at that time, amid the profiteers, the poor, and the gentlemen who vied with one another in regimental haberdashery, was a man who was to help to change the world. His name was Henry Bell, mill-wright and carpenter.

Bell did not make much of a living in Glasgow. He moved to the quiet town of Helensburgh on the Firth of Clyde. His wife took charge of the newly founded public baths there and she kept an inn. He was in business as a builder. Probably, he felt that there was little encouragement for the ideas he had tried to promote.

Twice he had submitted proposals to the Government for the building of ships driven by steam engines. On the first occasion, James Watt had not been impressed. Lord Nelson, however, was vigorously in favour, but he could not convince Whitehall.

Glasgow, in spite of the fact that it was powered to prominence as an industrial city mainly by the steam engine, was slow to recognise the value of steamships; its entrepreneurs and financiers delayed the development of them.

An outstanding engineer, called William Symington, had built an engine for a vessel which was tried on Dalswinton Loch in south-west Scotland. It was developed successfully and on two subsequent occasions his engines propelled small ships on the Forth and Clyde Canal. The second was the journey of the stern-wheel paddle steamer 'Charlotte Dundas' in 1802. The French and the Americans were already experimenting with this method of propulsion. They developed their own craft. But Glasgow did nothing. The 'Charlotte Dundas', the first dependable steamship ever operated, was immobilised because the directors of the Forth and Clyde Canal feared that her wash would harm the banks.

Nearly 10 years later, Bell crossed the Clyde from Helensburgh to Port Glasgow to persuade John Wood and Company to build him a ship—to be driven by his steam engine. Astronomers at the time were excited about a comet in the heavens. Bell called his little vessel 'Comet', and in January, 1812, she was launched and went through her paces like a thoroughbred. Six months later she was making three voyages a week on the Firth of Clyde, the first commercial steamship in the world to sail on open water, the little dark horse that started a dynasty.

Bell never made much money. The Clyde Trust, who governed the river, gave him an annuity of £100. Inventive engineers are too passionately complex for most people and their products are too easily taken for granted. The monuments to him were belated and skimpy. But in the 10 years after the launching of the 'Comet' 48 steamships were built on the Clyde.

The power of the steam engine was well established on land. Coal was plentiful. The Monkland Canal had been built, following a survey by James Watt, to bring barge-loads of it from the mines of North Lanarkshire. It was about 12 miles in length and was joined to the Forth and Clyde Canal at the barge docks of Port Dundas about one mile north-west of the city centre. These canals were in demand for the carriage of other goods and of passengers. The roads in those days were a perpetual object of complaint. Irrespective of delays at lock gates, transport by canal was often simpler and more convenient.

Even as the Napoleonic Wars were drawing to an end, preparations were being made to build Scotland's first vessel with an iron hull. It was to be the 'Vulcan', constructed not on the Clyde but on the Monkland Canal. The first ironclad steamer, the 'Fairy Queen', launched in 1831, was not built on the Clyde either. It was fabricated in Oakbank Foundry, Glasgow, and taken by road to the Broomielaw.

When the wars ended in 1815, the soldiers came home to a city of unemployment, deprivation, mass unrest, political intrigue, and cheap whisky. The town council despatched an address of congratulation to the Prince Regent after the victory at Waterloo. But it was not long before a different, hotter address for His Royal Highness was being vociferously recommended by thousands of angry workers as they marched through the streets.

The 'Corn Laws', introduced by Parliament to help the farmers by limiting imports, had raised the price of basic foodstuffs. A peck of meal cost about one third of an ordinary weaver's weekly wage. Tens of thousands were out of work. Demobilisation of sections of the army and the influx of hordes of hungry Irish into Glasgow made the sour and steaming chemistry of the place more critical.

A special relief fund, instituted by the Lord Provost in 1816, raised £9653 for distribution to 23,130 people considered to be 'in want'. Nearly twice as many people, however, gathered at Thrushgrove, outside the city, that winter to pass resolutions against the Prince Regent and the Government because of the plight of the country.

The clamour was not only for jobs and stable prices but for votes for all at the age of 21. Parliamentary voting then was the privilege of only a few thousand men of property in Scotland. In fact, a handful of Glasgow, Dumbarton, Rutherglen, and Renfrew councillors elected the one M.P. for the whole area.

Government spies were active in Glasgow. One or two of them, at least, were allegedly commissioned by the M.P., the famous Kirkman Finlay.

Strikes, mill closures, murders, and riots were frequent. At meetings of the Chamber of Commerce, accusations were made that strike leaders or political agents had thrown vitriol in the faces of those who disagreed with them. The town council publicly deplored the 'spirit of insubordination' that was rife in the streets.

They were concerned about another kind of spirit. In a plea to the Government for help in the situation of near-anarchy, they referred to the aggravating effects of cheap spirits, which were then being distilled illegally to the north and west of the city.

In this lurid sub-plot of local history, the Government had to put a revenue cutter into service on Loch Lomond to stamp out the bootleggers who were operating along the southern and eastern stretches of the 'bonnie banks.' Gangs on horseback openly transported illicit whisky in defiance of the Customs and Excise officers. Women were sent to Glasgow from the village of Balfron, 20 miles away, with whisky in tin vessels, strapped to their stays. The Campsie Hills and Fintry Hills in Stirlingshire were reeking with stills for years.

The manufacture of cheap, illegal whisky, fostered by Highland and Irish incomers in many instances, was inspired more by inflation than by shortage of retail outlets. In Glasgow at that time there were just over 1000 shops—and about 700 public houses or drinking dens.

Dr. Thomas Chalmers, the most famous presbyterian

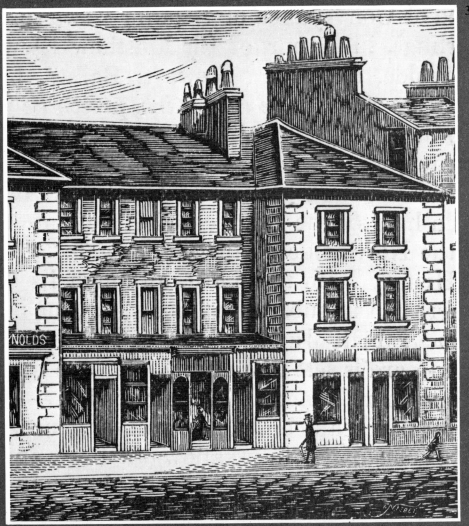

minister of the age, made thunderous speeches for 'twenty more churches and twenty more ministers.' Going beyond that, he demanded sweeping social reforms. He organised schemes for the relief of the poor and, because of fiery eloquence and his national reputation, he forced the town council to provide a new system of parochial schools for children of all classes.

The unrest, provoked by dire poverty, was so acute that some statesmen and industrialists feared a revolution such as the one in France 25 years earlier. Earl Grey said in the House of Lords: 'Glasgow was one of the places where treasonable practices were said, in the report of the secret committee of both Houses (of Parliament), to prevail to the greatest degree; but there can no longer be any doubt that the alleged treasonable oaths were administered by hired spies and informers.'

The efforts of the spies and informers on both sides produced distorted and bizarre information. Samuel Hunter, the plump and autocratic editor of the 'Glasgow Herald', was so disturbed by some of the stories that he went to the town council to demand the re-mustering of the Glasgow Volunteer Sharpshooters, who had served in the Napoleonic Wars. He was given command. They kept themselves under arms for four years, apparently without having to fire a shot.

In the spring of 1820, however, they were called into the streets together with several other regiments of foot and the hussars. The reason was the display of a poster on the walls of Glasgow churches, calling on the population to take arms to regenerate their country. It was signed 'By Order of the Committee of Organisation for forming a Provisional Government.' It was April Fool's Day but the poster was taken seriously.

A curfew was imposed. Everyone had to be off the streets by seven p.m. The military, on patrol at night, had powers to arrest any groups of people, found standing together or walking after seven p.m., and treat them as disturbers of the peace. A reward of £500 was offered for information about the authors or publishers of the revolutionary poster.

Glasgow, it was rumoured, was to be captured and used as the regional capital of the 'Provisional Government'. English working class insurrectionists were already marching towards Falkirk to seize the Carron Ironworks, where the famous 'Carronade' artillery was made. Armies were coming from France to help in the 'liberation' and 5000 French troops were to camp on Cathkin Braes on the southern outskirts of Glasgow. These were the stories, some disseminated by Government spies and some by Republican fanatics, which contributed to the cruel fiasco of the 'Radical War'.

Two days after the proclamation, about eighty men mostly weavers and labourers gathered at night in the Fir Park, near Glasgow Cathedral. Swords, muskets and ammunition were issued and they set off next day to join forces with the English rebels at Falkirk. They were dismayed to find no sign of their allies. About half of the men made their own way home. The rest were camped at Bonnymuir when a large troop of the 7th Hussars swooped on them. They put up a fight in which nearly all of them were wounded. They were arrested and taken to Stirling Castle.

Eighteen were charged with high treason. Fourteen of them were from Glasgow. Two of the leaders, Andrew Hardie, an ancestor of Keir Hardie (father figure of the modern Labour Party) and John Baird, a weaver from the village of Condorrat, were executed at Stirling. The others were ordered to be transported to the colonies.

The roster of duped martyrs of the time included the name of the man who was said to have invented the purl stitch in knitwear. He was James Wilson, a 60-year-old weaver from Strathaven in Lanarkshire. He had been among 20 men who had left their village to join what they thought was the heroic radical struggle that had broken out in Glasgow. As they met no evidence of this along the way, they reconsidered and decided to return home. Wilson was arrested soon after he reached his cottage.

Convicted of high treason, he was hanged and then beheaded before a crowd of 20,000 in front of the jail at Glasgow Green on August 30, 1820. That event and the other executions at Stirling may have crushed the militant radicalism temporarily but they did nothing to cure the tendency to mob violence in Glasgow. It could be triggered off too easily in favour of misguided as well as righteous causes.

Amid all the sectionalism and rumour-mongering, there was even a fear that Glasgow was marching to invade Edinburgh. Lord Cockburn, the Scottish judge and reformer, described the outcome in 'Memorials of His Time'. He was in Edinburgh.

'The perfect facility with which a party of 40,000 or 50,000 weavers could march from Glasgow, and seize upon the banks and the Castle of Edinburgh, without ever being heard of till they appeared in our streets, was demonstrated. Our magistrates, therefore, invited all loyal citizens to congregate with such arms as they had at various assigned posts.

'I repaired to the Assembly rooms in George Street with a stick about eight in the evening. The streets were as quiet as on an ordinary Sunday; but their silence was only held by the excited to forbode the coming storm. There seemed to be nobody abroad except those who, like myself, were repairing to their forlorn hopes.

'On entering the large room, I found at least 400 or 500 grown gentlemen, pacing about, dressed coarsely, as if for work, according to taste or convenience, with bludgeons, fowling pieces, dirks, cane-swords, or other implements. A zealous banker laboured under two small swivels, set on stocks, one under each arm. Frivolity, though much provoked and a good deal indulged in in corners, was reproved as unbecoming the crisis. At last, about 10 p.m., the horn of the coach from Glasgow was heard and the Lord Provost sent us word from the council chamber that we might retire for the night. We never met again.'

George IV, when he came to Scotland, enjoyed himself immensely at a great tartan durbar in Edinburgh. But he stayed well clear of Glasgow. Anti-Government feeling and the reputation of the mobs were too strong.

Scotland was going through a strange mood of ambivalence. There was the backward-looking romanticism about all things Scottish, typified by all the pageantry that accompanied the visit of the king and heavily influenced by the novels of Sir Walter Scott. At the same time, there was the forward-looking attitude of people who wanted to carry the country into a new age of prosperity with iron foundries and railways.

The earliest railway lines in the Glasgow area were for the carriage of coal and minerals generally. They were built in the 1820s. Associations of industrialists, merchants and town councils were formed to promote them in what became known as the era of 'joint stock mania'. Parliament was deluged by Bills and petitions about railways.

Glasgow's first station was St. Rollox in the northern part of the city. The line ran to Garnkirk in Lanarkshire and it was later extended to the town of Coatbridge. Like the one between Kirkintilloch and the coalfields of Monklands, opened about five years earlier, it was a commercial success almost immediately. Passenger trains were introduced on it.

Leading the city's affairs at the time were a few men who were among the most influential in its entire history. Kirkman Finlay and David Dale were survivors of a generation that had been directly influenced by Adam Smith. Finlay was head of the merchant house of James Finlay and Company, who opened up their own shipping routes to India and helped to smash the monopoly of the East India Company. In his lifetime, he was extremely popular—his murky role as a recruiter of spies for the Government before the 'Radical War' was not commonly known. He was M.P. for the area, Lord Provost of Glasgow, president of the Chamber of Commerce, Governor of the Forth and Clyde Canal and Lord Rector of the University all within 20 years. The only time he encountered popular disfavour was when he voted for the Corn Laws in Parliament, for which he was rebuked by a mob who smashed the windows of his house in his absence.

An important contemporary was Henry Monteith, who also became Lord Provost and was M.P. for the Lanarkshire group of burghs. He amassed a huge fortune in textile manufacture and dyeing processes. The improvement of the appearance of the city and the strengthening of its welfare services were among his main interests.

The two men came together with other like-minded citizens in a joint stock company to create a new residential area and main thoroughfare between Glasgow Cross and the northern perimeter of Glasgow Green. Before that the slopes between the riverside burgh of Anderston and the Cowcaddens had been the most flourishing area for new buildings. But the effect of the project, led by Finlay and Monteith, was to alter the balance of the city's expansion, eastwards instead of westwards, and to restore some of the residential character of the city centre.

Shares were taken by the town council, whose ideas about civic enterprise were far ahead of their time. Problems piled up around them. The population was growing at the rate of 25 to 35 per cent every ten years. It was the time when Scotland was discovering 'the radicalism of the stomach'. To help ease the unemployment, the council not only lobbied the Government for public works but commissioned novel schemes of its own.

One of these was devised to raise Glasgow Green to an elegance reminiscent of Vauxhall or, more appropriately, parts of Hyde Park in London. To an extent, they succeeded. They did it partly by public subscription and built driveways for horses and carriages. A contribution of £20 entitled the donor to a free ticket for life, no matter how many horses or vehicles he or his family cared to exercise there. The sum of £10 procured lesser privileges. All others, mounted or in carriages, had to pay tolls. In this way the capital was raised and work was given to the unemployed.

The struggle to maintain a decent, mixed environment was becoming ominously diversified. There were pressures on living space in parts of the city and across the river in Gorbals and Govan. Resources of coal and iron were being developed. The railway companies had to be prevented from acquiring ground along the Clyde which might be more profitably devoted to docks and shipbuilding.

The town council were facing momentous decisions which would set the pattern of the city's growth, correctly or incorrectly, for the next 80 to 100 years. In general, they responded bravely and wisely. It could not have been easy to consider long-term goals when short-term considerations included such items as purchasing more ground specially for the burial of the victims of typhus and cholera epidemics.

The joint stock promoters were claiming more ground than the dead and the deprived. The council steered well clear of a scheme to mine coal under Glasgow Green. They gladly endorsed railways to Edinburgh and to Greenock, but they blocked or successfully changed the plans for one or two other rail developments. By their actions, they managed to secure the banks of the Clyde, which had been further deepened in the late 1820s, between the Broomielaw and Port Glasgow, for shipping berths and, more importantly, shipbuilding. It is reasonable to argue that if they had not been so farsighted at the time, much of the raw materials and the trade of the area would simply have been carried away by the railways instead of being capitalised upon locally.

Ironworks had been founded within a few miles of Glasgow before the end of the 18th century. During the Napoleonic Wars when there was a large demand for cast-iron in making cannons, David Mushet, manager of the Calder Ironworks, had discovered big seams of blackband ironstone in Lanarkshire. But the man who brought about really spectacular developments was

James Beaumont Neilson, foreman and then manager of the Glasgow Gas Company. Around 1827-8 he conducted experiments in the use of waste gases and hot air in the blast at the furnaces. When he patented the process, there was a combination of good quality coal and low-grade ore which made 'Scotch pig-iron' cheaper and more plentiful than in any part of Britain. In the ten years between 1830 and 1840 the number of blast furnaces rose from 27 to about 100 and output multiplied tenfold.

Neilson, still a relatively young man, did not exploit the 'hot blast' invention by himself. Needing capital, he disposed of part of the interest in his patent to a local syndicate. He was a working man, born in Shettleston and raised in the Gorbals. After being employed as an engine-wright, he had taken up employment with the company who introduced gas lighting to Glasgow in 1818. His studies of chemistry and physics, allied to his engineering knowledge led him into a series of experiments which culminated in the 'hot blast'.

The syndicate, of which he was a member, comprised Charles Macintosh, Colin Dunlop of Tollcross, John Wilson of Dundyvan, and a lawyer who was employed as secretary of the group. Within a decade or so the process was in general use throughout Europe, the United States and India. The patent holders collected one shilling a ton from all that production. In the rush to get into the mass production of iron, a number of manufacturers tried to infringe the patent. In every case, they were defeated by the syndicate, either by legal action or threat of it.

A powerful consortium of ironmasters was formed to try to smash the patent monopoly. They spent hundreds of thousands of pounds. Seven major cases were raised, four of which were pursued all the way to the House of Lords, the supreme court of appeal in Britain. Many of the most famous industrialists and scientists of the age were called as witnesses. But the syndicate held for a long time.

Neilson, a quiet, humorous man with an odd, physical resemblance to James Watt, had plenty of money and a large family by the time he chose to retire and live on his country estate in his late fifties.

As the strength of industry was increasing and transforming whole areas within a few years, the strength of local government was declining. Scotland was emerging from a fairly long period in which the political regime and the judiciary had been incompetent and corrupt. Trials for high treason had been conducted, not so much as due process of law, but as deterrents to a discontented population, whom no town council could control, far less assuage.

Textile workers had been prohibited from forming official trade unions. The courts had found in favour of their masters. Radicalism, in its more extreme demonstrations, was as recurrently infectious as typhus or cholera. Nationally, the people wanted reform of Parliamentary elections. In the city, they wanted an end to the town council being drawn only from the ranks of the burgesses on a somewhat self-perpetuating basis.

Glasgow was possibly fortunate in the calibre of its civic leaders at that time. Their civic housekeeping as well as their foresight far excelled the average. By the early 1830s the cities of Aberdeen and Dundee had been declared bankrupt. Edinburgh, the capital, had largely irrecoverable debts of more than £400,000. But Glasgow, already considerably larger than Edinburgh, had kept down its debt to £78,000.

When the Parliamentary Reform Bill was introduced, the trades of the city organised an enormous demonstration with bands and banners. One or two contemporary accounts say that 150,000 attended it. Their slogan was: 'The Bill, the whole Bill, and nothing but the Bill'.

But they had to wait. The House of Lords opposed it. The following year, 70,000 gathered on Glasgow Green to support the sending of an address to the King, beseeching him to take measures for the passing of the Bill unamended.

When it was approved less than a month later, the city of Glasgow became entitled to send two members to the House of Commons. There were only 7,024 qualified voters, drawn not only from the city but also the suburbs of Gorbals, Calton and Anderston. As for the secret ballot, a list was published in the newspapers the following week showing how each man had placed his two votes.

In many ways, the reform of town councils was much more steadfastly and indignantly pursued. The problems were more immediate and evident. The Burgh Reform Act was passed in 1833 and on Guy Fawkes' Day that year, an extremely wet day, the first election was held. The city was divided into five wards with six councillors for each ward. In addition, there were two non-elected members, the Dean of Guild and the Deacon Convener of the Trades House.

Considering all the radical furore that had gone before and all the legislative tasks that lay before them, the first meeting of the freely elected town council (although there were probably only 8000 enfranchised out of a population of about 204,000) was a fiasco. The election of Robert Graham of Whitehill as Lord Provost apparently caused little trouble. But there was a row about whether the bailies should continue with the 'buffoon-like appearance' of cocked hats and gold chains. Then there was a more acrimonious squabble when the traditional glass of wine for each councillor was served at the close of formal business. Five of the new members walked out, decrying waste of money and unworthy drinking habits. Temperance was there and then enshrined, if it had not been already, as a perennial political issue of the Victorian age in Glasgow.

The city became a symbol of that age. As the tall chimneys rose like a congestion of organ pipes, there was the eternal and sonorous counterpoint of dynamic capitalism and social reform. There were marvellous and conflicting themes; but, more importantly, there was confidence, almost arrogance and a sense of adventure again.

Among any collection of outwardly douce, shrewd

business men there were always gamblers. Henry Monteith, usually renowned as a cautious, conservative man, pulled off a few notable gambles in the course of a career in which he gathered a gigantic fortune. On a smaller scale, he entered into wagers with his contemporaries every week. They were usually for bottles of rum. He laid a bet with a town councillor on the width of the jail. He accepted a bet that he could not make a noise like a cow louder than Mr. James Dennistoun, merchant and banker.

Charles Macintosh, who gave his name to the raincoat, was a scientist and entrepreneur who successfully backed Neilson in the development of the ' hot blast ' process. But he refused to support Napier's sea-going steamships because, he said, they were ' bound to fail '.

One of the most colourful of the tough tycoons was William Dixon, the ironmaster, who made a disastrous gamble when trying to introduce the Bessemer steel-making system. Nevertheless, he was a rich ironmaster, founder of 'Dixon's Blazes', just south of the Gorbals.

In his lifetime, he gained the reputation of being either the author or the object of more civil litigation than any man in Scotland. He sued or appealed from one court to another for years. One day when a case was called in the Court of Session, Lord Eldin, the judge, cried: ' Mr. Dixon again ? I protest—he should get a Lord in Ordinary (judge) tae himsel'.'

Dixon trusted his own judgement. When he took umbrage at the Clyde Navigation Trust because they would not carry his coal and iron by ship to Greenock at what he considered fair rates, he said: ' Damn them, I'll build a railway.' Many people told him that a railway alongside a waterway was a ludicrous idea. But he built it, and after it opened in 1840-41 it gave rise to competitive struggle between the railways and the passenger steamers.

Transport in the early 19th century had been a fairly limited choice for the Glasgow traveller; there were passenger vessels on the canals, stagecoaches and, for the more affluent, private coaches with fancy names, such as Dennets, Whiskeys, Stanhopes, Tilburgs or Droskys. Now there were steamers—small, shallow-draught steamers everywhere, frisking around the Firth of Clyde like a regatta of demented chimney pots. Companies competed on the same routes. They competed with the railway companies. Some joined forces with the railways to offer a joint service and then found themselves facing other combinations as rivals.

Races between rival steamers on the same route, much to the enjoyment of many passengers, were almost a daily occurrence on the estuary. It was too exhausting for some of the railway companies, who did not tend to stay long in the business. The competition was so keen that the fare from Glasgow to Rothesay on the Isle of Bute, which had been sixpence in the earliest years of the steamers was cut to threepence at one time.

Places like Rothesay, Dunoon and Millport prospered as a result of the great steamer profusion. The wealthier Glasgow people built houses there as holiday homes. As the Victorian age advanced, there were business men who commuted by train and passenger ship every working day. Old drawings and photographs show lines of coaches and rigs at Dunoon and Rothesay piers, awaiting the arrival of the evening ferry to take the company directors and lawyers to their homes.

Among the industrial giants, who were beginning to build handsome villas, even castles, for themselves on the shores of the Firth, the Bairds of Gartsherrie were the family who usually went one better than the rest. They bought vast estates in various parts of Scotland, in one case simply because the hunting was so good.

The Bairds were a squad of brothers. The family had been farmers turned coal miners in Lanarkshire. But the brothers were not content with the big dividends from coal. They went on to build iron furnaces and railways all over North Lanarkshire, controlled from their head office in Glasgow.

James Baird bequeathed £20,000 for ' Christian and charitable purposes ', a large sum in those days—but three years before his death he had given £500,000, in a deed of trust, to the Church of Scotland.

Towards the middle of the 1800s the rich were becoming richer. The poor were simply becoming more numerous. The devastating famines in Ireland caused thousands to migrate to Glasgow. If they were lucky enough to find work, it was likely to be in labouring jobs on the railways or on construction sites.

Records of wage rates in the lower paid jobs show that they scarcely changed at all in the decade up to 1851. Cotton spinners had their hours cut from 69 to 60 but their pay remained at 21 shillings a week. Labourers received only about a fifth of the wages of the highest paid, who were the iron rollers and puddlers at 8s to 13s 6d a day. This was the time when the development of malleable iron, as distinct from cast iron, was subject to intensive demand and skilled workers had to be tempted away from the north of England and the Midlands.

The continuing mixture of working class people from different origins created dissensions, some that were political and some that were not. The Chartist Movement was strong in the West of Scotland and the fires of more acute radicalism still burned in the older parts of Glasgow.

The year 1848 is famous for the number of uprisings in many parts of Europe. In that almighty, dissonant chord, Glasgow struck its own note.

Talk of revolution had been heard again. The bodies of Hardie and Baird, executed in the ' Radical War ' of 1820, had been transferred from Stirling Castle to a shrine in Glasgow Necropolis. An enormous crowd gathered on Glasgow Green on March 6, 1848 to march through the city, shouting ' Vive la Republique '. They clashed with the police and two military detachments for two days. Mills were damaged, shops looted, and by the time the streets had been cleared at least six people had been killed and many more injured.

PREVIOUS PAGE: *Locomotives that hoisted Glasgow to new levels of industrial fame. They were shipped to all corners of the world. There were engines with simply numbers, engines with names of thoroughbreds and engines that were plainly called 'puffing Billies', which pulled the others through the streets.*

OPPOSITE: *As the prosperous spread themselves in the 19th century, the architects planned good and gracious terraces and squares. They set new objectives.*
1 *Park Circus.*
2 *George Square, 1828.*
3 *The ornate plans for the west side of St. George's Cross.*

Chopin did not play the 'Revolutionary Etude', although the spirit of it was the theme of the times, on that cool, autumn afternoon of 1848 when he entertained in the Merchants' Hall. Two murders had been committed in weavers' strikes in Glasgow. The newspapers were full of reports of the trials of Chartists in London. It was a different world, though few could see that.

In front of a disappointingly small audience, mainly of wealthy people whose carriages filled Hutcheson Street, he rambled through the nocturnes. One critic was unkind enough not only to call his music 'novel, pathetic and difficult' but to point out that he appeared to have a weak constitution. Chopin had not wanted to play in Glasgow. But he needed the money. He was extremely ill and wanted to go home.

In these troubled times Queen Victoria disdained to follow the example of George IV and steer clear of Glasgow because of the danger of mobs or of demonstrations. In the following summer, she sailed imperially up the Clyde and into the heart of the city aboard the Royal Yacht. Crowds lined the river and the streets to see her. Victoria, who knighted the Lord Provost before coming ashore, approved of the city. She visited the Cathedral, the university, and the splendid new Queen Street Station, terminus of the Glasgow-Edinburgh railway. Both Victoria and Prince Albert expressed their admiration for the wide streets, flanked by new buildings.

If the builders and architects who were present at that evening's banquet felt satisfied, they had every reason to be. For the sober but increasingly culture-conscious middle class, sitting around them, they were providing houses of quality and a decent element of style. A school of handsome, in some cases distinctly elegant, urban architecture was beginning to show itself.

Glasgow was spreading to the north and west in a series of good and gracious terraces and squares. The people of propriety and prosperity were rising above the smoke, moving out towards Blythswood and Woodside. From the tall houses there, it was possible on a fine day to look out to Ben Lomond or the uplands of Renfrewshire; or, on a lower plane, look down on the paraphernalia of shipping and shipbuilding developments along the Clyde.

The city, by Act of Parliament, had more than doubled its size by annexing the three independent burghs of Anderston, Gorbals and Calton. Other suburban areas, left outside it, were not slow to take advantage of a later Act of Parliament and become independent burghs. Partick, Maryhill, and Govan led the way in gaining their own town councils and powers of local government. There was a great deal of squabbling about land-grabbing and the sharing of public services. It was one of the consequences of economic growth and, to a lesser extent, the wider freedom of political expression.

Links with America, founded by the aggressive trading of the tobacco merchants and others in the previous century, were profoundly influential in stimulating Glasgow's astonishing climb to fortune in the Victorian age. When Sir Robert Peel said in 1837 that he doubted whether, among all the cities on earth, there was one so 'remarkable for the combination of commercial and active industry and services rendered to science and literature as Glasgow', he was exercising a politician's flattery. Twenty years later that statement was nearer the truth. It was in the forefront of science and technology. It boasted a prestigious university, Britain's first technical college (Anderson's Institution, founded in 1796), a commercial college, an art college and a cluster of less formal centres for whole or part-time education, that were turning out masses of people with mechanical abilities well above average.

The Clydeside engineer had become an internationally recognised figure—and, obviously, on the credit side of humanity's anthology of species. His evolution is puzzling in some ways. There had been no long tradition of inventive skills with machinery. Other urban areas of Britain or Europe had superior pedigrees in that respect.

If there was a common picture of him, it was probably of a small, dark man with a grimy rag, hanging from a pocket of his overalls; a canny man, subject to occasional bouts of bad temper about the incompetence of others and possessed of a greater store of academic knowledge than his manners or his accent might suggest. He would turn or buff a piece of metal on the spot to make your broken down compressor function again; he would improvise marvellously with any materials at hand to re-jig a valve and get your ship across the China Seas. Quality of workmanship was learned, but adaptability was bred into him.

The transition from sail to steamships, which was a fairly slow process, was effected mainly through the builders and marine engineers of the Clyde. At the start of the 1850s, when many owners were still investing in ocean-going clippers largely because they had more capacity below decks, about 80 per cent of the steamships built in Britain came from the Clyde, which still launched far less tonnage each year than the shipyards on the Wear in North-East England. But in the next 20 years Clydeside became the largest shipbuilding centre in the world.

David Napier had not been put off by the fact that he never received payment for his work in Bell's 'Comet'. He and his cousin, Robert Napier, forged an empire for themselves by sheer enterprise and hard work, in the face of persistent scepticism about steamships. Robert had persuaded Samuel Cunard and others that, if they wanted to initiate a mail packet service between Britain and America, the ships they contemplated were too small. He built them bigger ships that soon became a byword in ocean travel under the flag of the Cunard Line. That was the start of a dynasty extending over 120 years in which the Clyde produced many of the greatest liners in the world, including the 'Queen Mary', 'Queen Elizabeth', and 'Queen Elizabeth 2'.

The tradition of building warships also started in the mid 1800s. Robert Napier, whose yard in Govan was

Queen Victoria

Chopin

booming, supplied what were considered startling designs for the 'Erebus', a floating battery, constructed in the incredibly short time of three and a half months for the Crimean War. He also built the 'Black Prince', a 6000-ton armoured frigate, and soon foreign governments were lining up to place orders for fighting ships.

Competition was furious. There was an eternal race to create bigger engines, better hull designs, and more passenger capacity for merchant fleets. From within the early ranks of the Napiers had come their main rivals. David Tod and John McGregor, who had worked for David Napier, had founded their own shipbuilding and ship-repairing business. John Elder, who had been in charge of Robert Napier's drawing office, quit to join forces with Charles Randolph and establish what eventually became the world-famous shipyard of Fairfield's. An even more famous yard, John Brown's of Clydebank, was the crowning accomplishment of two brothers, James and George Thomson, who had served Robert Napier as foremen. They created a town because it was the presence of their shipyard (named after their first venture, the Clyde Bank Foundry in Glasgow) and later the building of the Singer Sewing Machine factory there that formed Clydebank's identity.

Money was plentiful. Wages had been rising to such an extent that some of the banks, which in the 1850s were perpetually vying with one another to open more branches and raise more palatial head offices, found it worthwhile to cater for the working class by extending their hours of business two or three nights a week. Then one of them crashed, ruining hundreds of firms and many more individual investors.

The abrupt demise of the Western Bank, which had 101 branches throughout the country, was due to a failure by its management to interpret some of the sombre portents of the time. Too much money had been loaned to four large Glasgow companies, who, in turn, appeared to have been allowing their customers over-generous credit. Both they and the Western Bank had been deploying money in America without proper regard to the political and commercial instability there in that period before the Civil War.

When the war began, four years later, its effects were too severe for some of the textile companies, who had already suffered setbacks in the bank failure. As the main ports of the Confederacy were blockaded and raw cotton left to rot in the plantations, supplies diminished, prices soared.

Glasgow-based businesses, who commanded the fashionable end of the cotton goods market, were reputed to employ about 200,000 full-time and part-time workers in the West of Scotland and Northern Ireland. When Scottish imports of raw cotton fell from 87,000 tons a year to only 360 tons (between 1861 and 1864) they were forced to close mills, print shops, and dyeworks, paying off thousands of workers. It is fair to note that many of these were women and young girls, who undertook piece-work in their own homes. The local textile industry,

too heavily reliant on cotton, never recovered from the wounds it received in the Civil War. Imports, of course, became available again, but by then too many of the old guard were prepared to leave it to Lancashire to get on with the job and too many workers had dispersed.

Fashions were changing. The fabrics used in everyday dress were different, except for the poor. The fabric of society was vastly altered, except for the poor.

Glasgow was like a little New York in the brash, pioneering days of the passenger steamships. No Statue of Liberty stood at the Clyde gateway, petitioning: 'Give me your hungry . . .'. But they came, anyway. They arrived from the Western Isles of Scotland, looking for sea-going jobs or work in the shipyards. A small number, notably Italians and some Jewish migrants, came from Europe. Mostly, however, the incomers were from Ireland.

In the latter half of the 1800s it was commonplace for 10 to 20 per cent of the population at any one time to be Irish-born. With the single fare from Belfast fourpence to one shilling, it was the way of all underfed flesh.

The population grew at a faster rate than possibly any other part of Britain. Compared with modern statistics, the birth rate was fantastic—between 37 and 42 births for every thousand people—and it outstripped the death rate, even though that was still fairly high.

The average density of population became as crowded as 97 people to an acre. In the city centre for a long time it was at least 400. Most of the newer cemeteries allocated space at the rate of 70 to an acre.

Parts of a city inter-act on one another like cells in a complex organism. Glasgow was undergoing rapid mutations. More affluent houseowners, who had lived in the old Saltmarket, Anderston, or the area east of the Cathedral had tended to move to Blythswood or the better parts of Gorbals. But they now found commercial developments encroaching on their homes. They went elsewhere, usually to the west end or the new residential districts south of the Clyde.

The march of shipyards and shipping quays along the river was followed by the construction of row upon row of new tenements for the workers. Older tenements (many poorly ventilated, without damp courses in the walls), particularly in the city centre were congested and insanitary. Terrace houses, which had been sub-divided, were often just as foul. A system of 'ticketing' was introduced, whereby apartments were inspected, measured, and a ticket posted beside the door, giving their cubic capacity and prescribing the number of persons, over the age of eight, allowed to sleep in them. But people continued to sleep in lobbies (hallways) or on landings. When the police came to inspect, after midnight, they were known to hide temporarily on roofs or in other houses.

A gigantic programme of reform was required. Glasgow was a wealthy city. Politically, it was a Liberal city. Although generously favoured by some of its merchant princes and industrialists, it still suffered woefully from

The surprising grace of the public parks, cast around generously like bouquets among the red sandstone and the grey.
1/2 *Rouken Glen.*
3/4 *The interior and exterior of the Kibble Palace in the Botanic Gardens.*

the social evils of the free enterprise system at its most rampant.

Water was brought from Loch Katrine in the Trossachs of Perthshire, one of the greatest municipal services ever accomplished in Britain. That was followed, in 1866, by the formation of the City Improvement Trust, which gave the town council powers to eradicate slums and build new tenements, either for sale or rent, to house the working class. The creation of new parks and gardens, started in the 1850s, was expanded. Other benefits were extended— gas lighting, better sewerage, bathing facilities, and wash-houses.

All in all, it was a commendable drive to elevate the quality of life, a testament to the strength of community spirit at a time when old social groupings were disintegrating or being transformed with bewildering speed.

However, it was scarcely enough to keep pace with the earth-shaking movement of events. The iron railways were drilling through the ' drumlins ' to new suburbs and new docks. Glasgow had become one of the major centres of locomotive-building in the world. Underwater blasting finally smashed through the Elderslie rock, allowing further deepening of the Clyde and the passage of the biggest ships then afloat into the heart of the city.

In the 1870s the coming of steel ships—and, possibly more important, the brilliant Glasgow inventions in steel boilermaking—attracted more orders and more trade to the Clyde. The opening of the new route to the East through the Suez Canal had already sharpened the commercial appetites of the shipping companies.

The romance of the big ships will never be recaptured. Nor that of the douce Scots argonauts who operated them; stern-looking, bewhiskered gentlemen in dark clothes (as old photographs show them) and most of them knowing the inside of a deckhouse as well as they knew their gleaming mahogany and picture-lined head offices in Glasgow. Their demands were heavy, their sense of competition was acute, and their captains were like kings.

The bulk of their trade was with the United States and Canada. But their ships also went to South America, New Zealand, Australia, the Far East, Africa and the Mediterranean. The Anchor Line, the Donaldson Line, the Allan Line, the City Line, the Clan Line—they criss-crossed the globe. They were primarily responsible for making the phrase ' Clyde-built ' a kind of superlative in the international vocabulary because they usually bought their ships at home.

Emigration accounted for a big share of their passenger traffic across the Atlantic in the 1870s. The Canadian Government's offer of 160 acres free to anyone who would build a homestead and settle there attracted thousands of Scots. It is likely that Glaswegians were among them; it was at that time that an estimated one-sixth of the houses within the city were being demolished and the number of people leaving showed a marked increase.

Paralysis of the clearance and re-building set in when the City of Glasgow Bank failed in 1878. Financially, the consequences of this collapse were twice as bad as that of the Western Bank, although the long-term effect on industry and commerce was less harmful. In the days after the Bank closed its doors, companies in Manchester, London and Glasgow toppled. It was described three years later, when the task of liquidation had been largely completed, as ' the greatest disaster that had ever befallen the commercial community of Great Britain '.

A special relief fund was launched with the assistance of the Lord Provost and leading citizens. As bankruptcies piled up, schemes of public works were organised for the unemployed. Soup, bread, coal and money were doled out to them.

Mismanagement and fraud had brought down the City of Glasgow Bank. Charges of fraud and the falsifying of balance sheets were successful against directors, who were shipowners, distillers, merchants and town councillors. About £6,000,000 had been lost or misappropriated.

The winter of 1878-79 was a cruel one. A tough, prolonged strike of shipyard workers, which brought them little or nothing, had harmed the city. Three weeks after the Bank closed its doors, there was an explosion in a colliery in Blantyre, just outside Glasgow, which cost the lives of more than 200 miners, the worst underground disaster in the history of Scotland. The city raised a relief fund for the suffering resulting from that, too.

The Victorians were immensely generous. In retrospect, some people may conclude that the priorities of their beneficence were in a muddled, misdirected order; but, when everything is taken into account, it can be said fairly that they gave enormous sums to charities, missionary bodies, schools and emergency funds for the relief of distress. Glasgow was a redoubtable and unsurpassed example of that kind of Victorianism. The people who could sustain themselves comfortably were great improvers.

Social behaviour was more comprehensively changed between the early and late 1800s than in any previous century. Churches and cultural societies were more influential because of the spread of religious and secular education. Much of the social recreation, particularly organised activities for young people, was centred on the churches. The Boys' Brigade, which became an international movement, was founded in Glasgow in 1883.

Seventy or eighty years had brought little change in the number of hours worked, but there was a wider difference between the best paid and the lowest paid in the working class. In the continuing enlargement of the city, people came to identify more closely with their own district or neighbourhood. As evidence of what was probably a more serious-minded society, it could be seen that the old clubs were giving way to others of a determinedly improving or fashionable nature.

In the days before the growth of public halls and theatres, Glasgow had sported an array of social clubs (usually for men) which sparkled like a string of coloured lanterns through the long, Scots winter nights.

From a 19th century account, here are the names of

some of them with quotations about their characteristics. The Hodge Podge Club (' Originally of the literary order, but latterly degenerated to sixpenny whist '). The Face Club (' Partaking of sheep's head dinners was its *piece de resistance* '). The Coul Club (each member was accorded a mock knighthood on admission and addressed as ' sir '). The Gegg Club (composed of mischievous, well-off young men—' After a few hours of song and sentiment, they generally wound up the evening with some practical joke, such as locking a nightwatchman in his box or overturning it on top of him '). The Shuna Club (' This somewhat aristocratic organisation, which was conducted very much on the " pies and porter " principle '). Others were called Rumble Gumpy, the Beggars' Benison, Dirty Shirt, and the Driddle. They appear to have been lively.

The Victorians were less disposed to patronise them. Prestige, monuments, public causes, the stuff of history—these loomed much larger. They were eager to honour their great and successful men. And, truly, there were giants in those days.

William Thomson, later Lord Kelvin, was one of them. Born in Belfast, he entered Glasgow University at the age of 12 and 10 years later became a professor there. His scientific studies of heat and energy, notably those about electricity, earned him international respect. During an extraordinarily long career, he carried out the proving work which led to the laying of the first Atlantic cable, and for that he was formally honoured by the city. Lord Kelvin was responsible for fostering major advances in scientific activity at the university and, later, the development of electrical engineering industries in the area.

Another notable scientist was James Young, who had started his adult life as a carpenter and then attended Anderson's College. He exemplified the kind of self-made man Glaswegians most respected. Young was the first man successfully to produce naphtha, lubricant oils, kerosene and solid paraffin from coal and subsequently from shale.

Joseph Lister, professor of surgery, was the principal discoverer of antiseptics. Taking inspiration from Pasteur, he proceeded through a series of painstaking experiments in a Glasgow hospital before achieving a usable form of carbolic.

Glasgow still had too many people, too much susceptibility to boom or bust; but its pride was reaching as high as its buildings. Sculptors, makers of commemorative plaques, writers of gilded scrolls, and newspaper editorialists were thriving. Mr. Gladstone came to pay tribute to all the industrial enterprise around him. Mr. Disraeli came to pronounce on higher things when he was installed as Lord Rector of the University in 1873. He showed more composure than his illustrious predecessor, Edmund Burke, nearly a century earlier, who, in the same circumstances, broke down after five minutes, saying he could not continue because he had never addressed so learned an audience.

The university by the time Disraeli was installed had moved from the Old College near the Cathedral to Gilmorehill above the river Kelvin. When the old buildings were largely swept away, a railway—inevitably—came thundering through the site. There was a good deal of controversy because some of them had been of high architectural quality. Lord Cockburn, the judge, sniffed that the main reason for the transfer of the university was the selfish desire of the professors to get better houses in the west end.

The city undoubtedly had a habit of eradicating its architectural beauty spots and preserving the warts. Some truly elegant houses disappeared in rubble beneath the wheels of the iron cars of Victorian progress.

By the 1870s the iron cars were in the streets. The tramways had begun just like the railways—a plurality of companies, hectic competition, advertisements that read more like the blandishments of circuses than public services and a whole cavalcade of noise and colour that became a daily feature in the lives of three or four generations. Even though the town council imposed a governing hand on the development of the tram routes at a fairly early stage, they cheerfully meandered here, there and everywhere. No line was too speculative, no service too troublesome, and no idea too impracticable. There were horses at particular staging posts. There were even steam trams for a time, almost driving householders mad with their din and dirt. Eventually, they were powered by electricity and run by the town council.

Glasgow fell in love with them. It became possibly the greatest tramway city in Europe. The system was certainly the cheapest and most serviceable in Britain. The noise of a double-deck tram at night, careering down Argyle Street or London Road like a runaway house on fire, was as familiar as the daytime metallic clatter of the shipyards. They were painted with bands of colour as destination codes. There were blue trams to Clydebank, yellow trams to Langside, and green trams that carried the locomotive workers to and from Springburn. Along 270 miles of track—there always seemed to be a tram in sight. A common vein of the nostalgia of older generations is that the trams were so dependable.

Twenty years before the tramways were electrified, electric lighting was introduced at two of the main line railway terminals. That was in 1879 when there were five such terminals.

The red carpets were frequently unrolled in them. As Glasgow's industrial strength became more widely known abroad, the rich and the famous came to visit it. Indian rajahs, members of the Japanese royal family, Chinese statesmen, and the Shah of Persia brought their shopping lists. They wanted ships, locomotives and machinery.

The Grand Duke Alexis of Russia gabbled excitedly that Glasgow was ' the centre of intelligence of England ' when he came to the launching of the ' Livadia ', the royal yacht of the Czar. When it was completed in 1880, it was one of the strangest ships afloat, designed by

1/4 *In retrospect, the trams seemed to fit appropriately into the Victorian architecture—rattling along on wires like old-fashioned cash-carriers in a bustling emporium of empire.*
5 *Progress called for the removal of the old university buildings near the Cathedral.*
6 *The buildings which replaced them in the 1870s, sited on Gilmorehill, above the River Kelvin.*

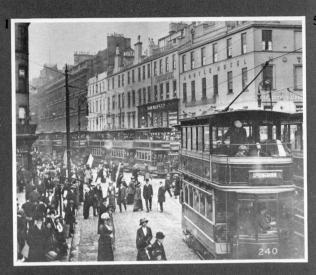

Admiral Popoff of the Russian Navy with an assortment of stablisers which guaranteed, among other things, that billiards could be played aboard, even in rough weather. It was exactly the kind of modern convenience that would appeal to the sporting and technical instincts of the Clydesider, but it was never proved.

Local potentates, who were widening their tastes as well as their fortunes, indulged themselves in steam yachts, although less large and palatial. Naturally, they were Clyde-built. They lay at anchor at Cowes, or Cork, or in the Firth of Clyde during the ' Clyde Fortnight ' each summer, while the younger sons of the family took part in sailing races. The sport was less important than keeping up appearances. Steam yachts and motor cruisers and six-metre sailboats were the stuff of status.

The ' Lysistrata ', built for Mr. Gordon Bennett, an American, had a cycle track round the main deck. Another yacht, built for a Glasgow merchant, had a pipe organ aboard. The ' Hermione ', once owned by directors of the Allan Line for cruising in the Hebrides, found itself in the service of the U.S. Navy in the Spanish-American War and sank a Spanish ship by gunfire off Cuba in 1898. All the steam yachts of that period were fast, elegant vessels, the true and now extinct poetry of the shipbuilders.

The man who was responsible for much of the interior design of the outstanding exception, the ' Livadia ', was a Glasgow architect called William Leiper. He fulfilled another strange contract before that. According to the story, the owner of Templeton's carpet factory was dissatisfied with designs for new buildings. He asked his architect what was the finest building in the world. ' The Doge's Palace in Venice ' was the reply. ' Build it here ', he said. Leiper designed a replica in terra cotta, red brick and coloured mosaic which still stands on the north side of Glasgow Green.

Extravagant flourishes of Victoriana were plentiful. The new municipal chambers in George Square not only set the new centrepiece of the city but displayed the refined opulence that was in style in the 1880s, a desire to overlay wealth with grace—but not as much as to hide the wealth. In the ethos of it, there are whispers of ' look upwards and admire ' and ' just feel that marble '.

Glasgow has never been forgiven for smashing down great buildings. It removed Adam houses. It desecrated Georgian buildings by re-modelling. It abolished without much compunction the historic premises in which Lister first demonstrated antiseptic surgery. But Glasgow has also received world-wide commendation for the preservation of much of its outstanding Victorian architecture.

The architects of those days exemplified much more than native adaptability. They were originals, not rigidly subservient to local tastes or dominated by London fashions.

Charles Wilson laid out fine terraces. James Sellars was a master of subtle, enhancing detail in his big buildings. Alexander Thomson, consumed with a passion for distinctive arrangements of Greek and Egyptian ornament, challenged conformity and the damp climate with his masterpieces. J. J. Burnet, who as a youth had studied under Jean-Louis Pascal in Paris, was always versatile and hardly ever short of brilliant. And Charles Rennie Mackintosh, one of the prime movers in the Art Nouveau school, designed the world-famous Glasgow Art College and a succession of superb houses in Scotland, Austria and Germany.

Glasgow had good stone for its buildings. There was little of the fancy decorating of brick frontages, stucco camouflaging, or tricking out of windows and porches, which could be seen in other cities. Much of the stone was imported from a good many miles away, but some of it was quarried locally. In the heyday of the best Victorian construction there was a kind of Biblical sight in the streets as horses hauled blocks of it towards the sites.

In the west end, Pollokshields and the suburb of Bearsden, there were formed trim, regular boulevards that stretched away into the distance like guarantees of gentility and permanence. Meanwhile the configurations of the city centre were being changed by brilliant, dramatic interpolations of Burnet, Mackintosh and others.

Regularity but not elegance marked the working class districts. Tenements rose with barrack-like, military precision. Behind them and between them, almost in contrasting disorder, were assorted little workshops for casting, forging, engineering, carpentry and a mass of satellites of the big industries. The railways ran rings round them and all along the Clyde, within the city boundaries, was the spiky scenery of shipyards stocks and cranes. These working class districts were what a Victorian artist described as ' the un-getatable backlands that know no cab ranks '.

The trams took the people ' into town ' on a Saturday. The central area was thronged with socialising and recreation-seeking people, not simply shoppers as it is nowadays. Sauchiehall Street was ' uptown ' and salubrious. Argyle Street was ' downtown ' and commercial, the true pitch of the masses. There were street vendors, musicians, pavement artists, men selling second-hand books from barrows in alleyways, and horse-drawn brakes carrying football supporters, who exchanged banter with the crowds on the pavements as they passed slowly by. They were less rancorous, more jocular than the football supporters of today.

But in those days most workers served a five-and-a-half or a six-day week. Saturday, if you could claim all of it or most of it for yourself, was for happiness.

Glasgow, said an essayist, was ' a very Tokyo for tea rooms '. To judge by the profusion of them, they must have been popular. To judge by the politics and the expressions of social reform then, they were also favoured as an antidote to the heavy drinking habits. One of them demanded that all young women on the staff had to supply references from a minister of religion. The most famous of them was run by Miss Kate Cranston, who each day lined up the waitresses to inspect their underwear and ensure that it met her high standards of cleanliness.

The working class were spreading themselves. Men travelled farther to work. Little steamers called 'Cluthas' chugged up and down the Clyde like buses from the city centre to Whiteinch, three miles away, with eleven landing stages and a fare of one penny. The city began to make plans for an underground cable railway to facilitate passenger traffic backwards and forwards across the river.

Holidays at resorts on the Clyde coast or in Ireland became popular. The crowds for week-end excursions on the Firth grew larger. There was so much drunkenness on the steamers, because of the bars being open usually at different hours from the public houses ashore, that one owner introduced the 'Ivanhoe' as a 'dry' ship. For 17 years there was an engraved drinking fountain aboard, informing the passengers that they could go further but would fare worse. And for longer than 17 years a type of metal receptacle for the hip pocket was known colloquially in Glasgow as an 'Ivanhoe flask'.

Drunkenness was a problem. The magistrates, conscious of the political power in the temperance movement, were stern about the licensing of public houses. They took the view that conviviality in them must be discouraged. Too many seats in them, for example, were prohibited. However, their tactics probably were wrong and encouraged the stubborn 'perpendicular drinking' in an all-male environment which has been a blot on the city.

Accompanying the reduction of working hours, there was a widespread flowering of sports clubs. One of the first and most distinguished in association football, not simply in Scotland but in Great Britain, was Queen's Park F.C. which began in Glasgow in the late 1860s. They remain amateurs. Once it was a wealthy club, and its decision to build Hampden Park, with its vast accommodation for spectators, was in itself a testimony to the phenomenal growth of the game's appeal.

Rangers F.C., founded in 1873 mainly as an association of Protestant young men from the north and west of Scotland, was followed by Third Lanark, Clyde, Partick Thistle and Celtic. The game, in its organised form, had respectable, middle-class origins, but it may be claimed (with some hesitancy rather than spontaneous pride) that Glasgow taught the world football fanaticism. All the clubs that were founded in Victorian times, with the exception of Third Lanark, still compete in the major leagues. Dominance is held by Rangers and Celtic, largely because of the tradition of Protestant and Roman Catholic rivalry which has dogged them. Supporters have been known to state in their last will and testament that they wish to be cremated after their deaths and to have their ashes scattered on the playing fields of Rangers or Celtic.

Athletics, bowls, rugby, rowing, cycling and cricket clubs proliferated in the late 1800s. Older sports, such as curling and quoits, probably had many more players then than they have nowadays. In the days when the curlers still had open ponds within a mile or two of their offices, the golfers did not have far to travel, either. Two public courses and eighteen private courses lay within an eight-mile radius of the city centre.

More than the holes were numbered. Their days, in many cases, were numbered. The city was still spreading outwards and in 1891 it incorporated six formerly independent burghs and other lands on its outskirts.

Naturally, there was some resentment. Glasgow had already been accused of imperialism and 'creeping socialism' simultaneously. The town council assumed municipal control of public services, such as gas and transport, either earlier or on a bigger scale than most of its counterparts in Britain. Powers acquired for slum clearance, re-building, and the creation of open spaces were, in their day, decidedly *avant-garde*.

The whole fresco of life had widened in a way that would have been inconceivable eighty years earlier. Although it contained more variety and livelier forms of human activity, the space between the very rich and the poor had extended. Glasgow, second city of the Empire, was the powerhouse of Scotland.

At the start of the century it had accommodated one Scot in 20 within its boundaries. At the end of the century nearly one Scot in every five lived in Glasgow. Newspapers of the time frequently published long speeches by politicians or pundits, eulogising over its progress and climaxing with ringing assertions about how the best was yet to come. Handsomely-bound books were published, full of photographs and grand prose about marching into the 'Twentieth Century'. 'Look around . . . the most prosperous and populous of the northerly cities of the world.'

The winter of 1894-95 had been a reminder of the location. The Clyde had frozen again. In March, 1895, small steamers had been used as ice-breakers to create passage for the bigger traffic. One of them collided with a lighter and sank. Another small vessel also sank. Big passenger ships were dragged from their moorings in the docks by the ice. In the worst two weeks, at the end of February and the beginning of March, the death rate in the city was at the incredibly high rate of 51 to 54 for every 1000 of the population.

Underfed, badly-housed people could not stand the cold. When the Boer War came at the turn of the century the medical examination of prospective soldiers threw up so much information about the poor physical state of the population that recommendations were made by a board about preventive health measures and means of raising nutritional standards.

The deficiencies were obvious enough. There were many societies or agencies committed to assisting people in need. But it was not always easy to identify the most deserving cases. And the methods of some bodies, like the parish councils did not endear them to certain types of Scots who did not want to be seen begging for sustenance.

In the early 1900s there were more opportunities for wage earners. But there were many jobs with no lasting security; hire and fire were peremptory. Men in the steel

The unmistakable triumphs of Charles Rennie Mackintosh.
1 Glasgow School of Art.
2 Furnishings by Mackintosh, the comprehensive master.
3 His distinctive tea room in a city described as ' a very Tokyo for tea rooms.'
4 Inside the Glasgow School of Art.

53

industry could be laid off at a few hours' notice. Craftsmen in the shipyards could be dismissed as soon as their specific contribution had finished and then re-engaged a week or so later. Joiners there and on construction sites carried large boxes of tools on their shoulder as they hiked from one place to another, sometimes working for two or three employers in a couple of months.

Cheap, plentiful labour was one of Glasgow's major assets, not socially but certainly industrially. Even when Scottish ores expired and local coal became less of a worthwhile commodity in the steel works, which then had to import raw materials from further afield, the pool of labour helped to keep down costs.

The years between the late 19th and early 20th century, when working men became better informed and more organised, were critical in the history of the trade union movement. Glasgow became the centre of union activity in Scotland, headquarters of the Scottish T.U.C. Most of the employers' associations in the major industries also chose to have their headquarters in the city. Although they did not command any space in the handsomely-bound books of provincial Pooh-Bahs, many of the most influential and colourful figures of the time were union leaders and key men in employers' organisations.

The modern factory or assembly plant, full of different crafts and new species of semi-skilled labour, presented problems to the trades unions. In and around the city, such factories, which were not really similar to the old ' manufactories ' of the textile era, were multiplying. A few, large American companies were among those coming to Clydeside.

Although not all of the exports, shipped from the Clyde, were made in Glasgow, most of them were produced locally. Output, particularly from the heavy industries, soared. Between 1900 and 1913, the value of exports from Glasgow increased from £18m to £36m. America was one of the main markets.

Capital was also flowing out to America. The first significant Scottish investments in North America, Australia, and New Zealand had begun in the 1860s. By the end of the century, it had reached such a degree —particularly in the United States—that it later drew this comment from Professor W. Turrentine Jackson, of the University of California: ' Apparently the heavy industries of the Clyde no longer profitably utilised all of Glasgow's surplus capital. This may well be regarded as one of the most significant developments in Scottish-American relations between 1900 and 1914.'

Money was poured into agricultural mortgages, lumber, mining, railways, land reclamation and building. It was often raised at lower interest rates in Scotland than could be obtained in the eastern cities of America; it was poured into the country by companies like the Glasgow American Trust, the Glasgow Californian Land Company, West of Scotland American Investments and literally scores of syndicates with American titles. The great Jumper Gold Mine was exploited with Glasgow money. But on many other mining gambles the coalmasters, tradesmen and accountants back home lost heavily.

Too many were keen to invest abroad instead of in their native city. There was the example of the motor car industry. Naturally Scottish engineering was interested in it. Sir William Arrol, the bridge builder, and a few of his friends teamed up with an intrepid designer called George Johnston to build the Arrol Johnston car. Two of Johnston's former colleagues started the company which launched the Albions and out of Bridgeton came an engineer, Alex Govan, who designed and produced the most famous Scottish car, the beautiful, world record-breaking Argyll.

None of these models survive except as curios in museums or private collections, although the name of Albion is continued through the commercial vehicles they make as part of the British Leyland Motor Company.

The cars are relics of a romantic period when engineers with more ideas than money, working in sheds or small factories, brought out their revolutionary contraptions to disturb the rumbling, horse-drawn traffic, to make the ladies quite giddy in Kelvin Way, and terrify the chickens on the banks of Loch Lomond. Considering the inventiveness and adaptability of Glasgow engineering, the fact that the Scottish motor car industry lasted for only about 30 years is a mystery. But its early cantrips were scandalous and dashing.

The Suffragettes, demanding women's rights to vote on equal terms with men, cut a dash, too. They were perhaps not so dramatic as the women in London. They did not smash so many windows or stage as many marches, but in Glasgow they were fiercely articulate. Sunday night meetings at street corners were by then a well-established custom. The Suffragettes claimed their stances, banged the makeshift lectern with the best of them and snapped back at the robust heckling that was all the sabbath sport. Then they would go home on the tram, usually to ornate drawing rooms in Hillhead or Langside. Even that, at a late hour on a Sunday night in sombre, serge-suited Glasgow, was defiance in itself.

Women, of course, were beginning to infiltrate the heavy industries before the First World War. They had been employed in textiles for more than 120 years. But they were beginning to be seen in finishing trades, such as French polishing in the shipyards and furniture factories, and even as machine minders. It was a sign of the booming times.

The year 1914 was a turning point. By then the city's population was about one million because of the annexation (in 1912) of peripheral areas, including the burghs of Govan and Partick. Govan, simply swallowed by Glasgow, had been about the fifth largest town in Scotland. Partick, an independent-minded place with a good stock of skilled workers and families of Highland extraction, had gone down fighting. Tears had been shed at the valedictory gathering in the burgh hall. The great Highland air of ' Lochaber No More ' had been played on the organ. And then the last provost of the burgh had somewhat

Few cities have so hungered after sporting fame or feted its champions. Some sports may rise in popularity, others may fall; but the passion remains.
1 The end of the trail for thousands of club players—the Bowling Championships at Queen's Park.
2 The beginning of some of the rules of association football; a letter from the secretary of Queen's Park F.C., dated July 29, 1868, in which he suggests, among other things, that the two teams should change ends at half-time.
3 Rangers play Celtic, the greatest attraction of all.
4 The Queen's Park team of 1873–74. Each man was allowed to emblazon his jersey with his own choice of lion crest—like whiskers, it was a matter of personal taste.

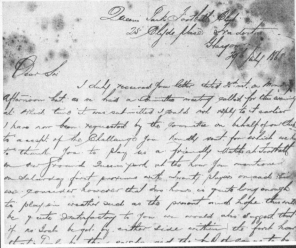

QUEEN'S PARK FOOTBALL CLUB

SEASON 1873-74.

(BACK ROW) A. McKINNON, J. DICKSON, T. LAWRIE, C. CAMPBELL, R. W. NEIL,
(FRONT ROW) R. LECKIE, J. TAYLOR, H. McNEIL, J. J. THOMSON, J. B. WEIR, W. McKINNON,

spoiled the occasion by proclaiming, as he cast his robes on a chair: ' There they lie—the abandoned habits of the last provost of Partick.'

The war, with its mobilisation of human resources on a scale never known before, brought profound changes. Women were in demand—for jobs in service industries to replace men, in munitions factories, and even in the shipyards. Shipbuilding, which had been prosperous before the war, attained its all-time peak of production. It was casting around, not only for women workers but for any men it could get from outside Clydeside. As men, who had never previously seen a shipyard, came in from the country to the city, others were moving out, transferring to jobs in armaments factories or, as it was described, ' work of national importance '.

Still more were dying—at Passchendale, the Dardanelles, Ypres, the Somme. It was not like the Boer War. The spindly boys from Bridgeton and Anderston went down with the fitter men from the good, residential districts. They wore the ensignia of famous Lowland and Highland regiments, hallowed with battle honours of Assaye, Inkerman, and the Napoleonic wars. Nobody surpassed their record as fighting men. The Glasgow soldier, in his grim way, achieved the same global respect as the Clydeside engineer.

The beloved Clyde steamers suffered casualties. Thirty-one of them were taken away for war service and five never returned. They carried troops to France, operated as naval tenders and minesweepers, and even saw battle. One of them rammed and sank a German submarine. Another returned to the Thames with a damaged Zeppelin at the end of a towrope.

During these years there was considerable social and political upheaval in Glasgow. The refinements of living in the pre-war era—the salubrious new buildings that were landmarks of growing prosperity, the Sunday promenades to hear the bands in the parks, the evening cruises on the river, and all the sailor-suited smugness that is still touchingly revealed in sepia photographs—all of these were rudely submerged or transformed.

' Rent Strikes ' were staged against alleged profiteering by landlords. More significantly, there was some opposition to conscription and strikes by workers engaged in the war effort. In some of the biggest industries, they fought against regulations curtailing wages and prohibiting workers leaving their employers for the duration of the war.

Clydeside was regarded by Whitehall as a dangerous breeding ground of Socialist subversives. Mr. Lloyd George came to address foundry workers and engineers, and was surprised by the hostile reception. Anti-war protesters held meetings at which there were often clashes with people who denounced them as unpatriotic. In the bloodshed (wooden batons and twelve-inch lengths of iron tubing were known to have been used) some of the casualties were dissidents who later became Government ministers, Lords and Privy Councillors.

The crusading passion of the working class leaders in Glasgow was not matched in its intensity anywhere else in Britain. Crowds attended the lectures on economics given by John MacLean, whom Lenin, after the Russian Revolution, created Soviet consul in Glasgow. In the Albion motor works, men gathered at lunch-time for educational classes, run by Willie Gallacher, later a Communist M.P. for West Fife.

Undoubtedly the greatest force was in the ranks of the Independent Labour Party. Their leaders were arrested and imprisoned, but they survived that and went on to become the most celebrated group of Parliamentary politicians that Scotland has ever seen.

The activists included schoolmasters, trade unionists and a few business and professional men. They were an assortment of intellectuals, strike organisers, flamboyant orators and hard-necked ward marshals from local politics. The names which survived most prominently were those of John Wheatley, James Maxton, David Kirkwood, John McGovern, Willie Gallacher, Tom Johnston, Emanuel Shinwell and George Buchanan. There were others whom political history has perhaps under valued. For a time, while their alliance lasted, their various talents formed exactly the right kind of appeal to many Glaswegians at that point in history—a combination of energy, eloquence, self-sacrifice and respect for learning.

When the war ended and women were given the vote, the victorious Suffragettes marched to Kelvingrove to plant a commemorative oak. But in the troubled territory of industry nobody was laying down the olive branch. Not that Clydeside had failed to serve the war machine; it had produced weapons, munitions and a record-breaking output of ships and it had good reason for pride.

In January, 1919, a huge demonstration, mostly of shipbuilding and engineering workers, was assembled in George Square. The normal working week was 54 hours and they wanted it reduced to 40. In a spell of nervous uncertainty while a deputation was attempting to secure a hearing of their case from the Lord Provost, police drew their truncheons and drove back some of the crowd outside the City Chambers. The fighting, brief but bloody, led to casualties on both sides. Kirkwood was felled by a truncheon and Gallacher was left bleeding and semi-conscious on the pavement.

A little lick of martyrdom went a long way. Only two Socialists had gained seats in the Parliamentary General Election of 1918. But in 1922 a cascade of popular support carried the I.L.P. group to victory in 10 of the city's 15 seats. Strong declarations of social justice were made, Socialist anthems and hymns were sung, and thousands of people escorted the new M.P.s to the railway station when they left to take their seats in the House of Commons. They carried the ideals of some and the vague hopes of many more.

All was not well in Glasgow for the bulk of the people. Men, returning from the war, had found jobs difficult to get. While it was still being fought, the town clerk of

Glasgow had stated in a speech that the city's unsurpassed diversity of industries made it immune from the threat of depression. But that had been a distorted echo of Edwardian-age confidence.

In the early 1920s shipbuilding slumped, although it picked up again towards the end of that decade. Engineering was starved of orders and for marine engineering, with the increasing development of oil fuel instead of coal, the prospects for the Clyde were shrinking because it had been slow to accept the new technology.

The pernicious unemployment that marked the inter-war years had begun. Even before the world depression after 1929-30 there were signs of weakening economic power. Companies in the West of Scotland were being taken over by larger, English concerns. Some Scottish banks came under English control. Too much of the profits from industry over 60 years had been transferred from Glasgow to overseas investments from which the yield in dividends or appreciation did not come back to source.

It was a strange decade of poverty and radicalism seeking expression, of a carefree post-war generation seeking new pleasures and of burgeoning middle-class ambitions seeking fulfilment in motor cars, bungalows, and most of all, a little bit of security and financial stability. New cinemas were built around the corner from slums. Department stores were selling dresses of the latest daring hem-line while, by the light of their window displays, limbless ex-servicemen drew with coloured chalks on the pavement. Past posters, stating that you, too, could have the last word in modernity in Acacia Avenue for £25 down, trudged the hunger marchers.

In Parliament, the firebrand M.P.s from Glasgow, who had gone there with the idea of overhauling the entire parliamentary system but never succeeded, made impassioned pleas about the need for social welfare services and remedies for bad housing and unemployment. John Wheatley, the only one to reach cabinet rank in the Government, was a moving force behind Labour's policies on housing reform. Maxton, brushing his lank hair off his brow, dramatically denounced the Government as murderers when they tried to cut the expenditure on health services in Scotland. Agitating, pleading, protesting, the Clydeside group were frequently in trouble, even to the extent of fighting with the ushers on occasions when their members were asked to leave the debating chamber.

In the Socialist ranks a caucus; in Parliament, a ruckus: yet they came from a city which, in their lifetime, had given Britain two Prime Ministers, Sir Henry Campbell-Bannerman and Mr. Bonar Law, an old guard Liberal and a Conservative.

The General Strike of 1926 only deepened the sense of economic uncertainty that gripped many people. But by then the foundations of a new future were, literally, being laid.

Glasgow was quick to take advantage of the Housing Acts, passed by Parliament in the early 1920s, which conveyed far-reaching powers and duties to the local authorities. The pioneering work in municipal housing, started in Victorian times, had already been strengthened when the Glasgow Corporation and Police Act (plus a subsequent item of legislation) transferred the old Improvement Trust, lock, stock and barrel to the town council, now Glasgow Corporation, with new borrowing powers and obligations. The Corporation had taken advantage of this to a limited degree. But it was not until the national legislation of the 1920s that they could implement sweeping plans for improvement.

Thousands of people were provided with new homes for rent. For those who had lived in one or two-room flats, these houses were little short of magnificent. Although some were built in a style similar to the traditional tenements, the majority were terrace houses or cottages, semi-detached houses or ' four-in-a-block ' flats within the semi-detached form of construction.

Many were built on the then periphery of the city. They caused the density of population to decline as Glasgow again spread itself into the neighbouring counties of Lanarkshire, Renfrewshire and Dunbartonshire. In fact, between 1926 and 1938 the area of the city more than doubled.

Another factor eased the density of population, less happily; emigration. In sheer volume of numbers, 1920-1930 was the era of the great exodus from Scotland. There were ample places to go. Before and after the zenith of the British Empire, in Victorian times, the Scots had established themselves everywhere that seemed environmentally suitable to their nature and customs or where they could exploit their talents, without compromising their sense of freedom and justice. They made outposts to which their own folk were always welcome, tea planters, mine managers, joiners and men off the boat.

The legacy of Victorian times, however, was the burden for the people at home. There were the heavy industries, among the first victims of the shortage of investment capital. There were the environmental and social problems of the overcrowded tenements that had outlived the manpower-mad days of ' throw 'em up and pack 'em in '.

Quite simply, Glasgow stopped growing. The size of the population stabilised.

The 1930s were cruel. Unemployment at the rate of 30 per cent was not uncommon. Shipyards and factories closed. Hunger marchers slept in the streets of Edinburgh and in other places on their way to London. The National Unemployed Workers' Movement could muster 100,000 people in the streets of Glasgow, as they did on at least one occasion. Elsewhere in Britain, new factories were still being started—2688 between 1932 and 1936—but hardly any of them in Scotland's major industrial city.

If a man worked on a municipal building site, he was envied. Too many men were passing the time playing dominoes in public halls or church halls, or taking part in the organised country walks and hill-climbs that were among the folk-fashions of the 1930s. In one part of the

Glasgow keeps changing, occasionally surprising itself. It is a consciously functional city with expanding motorways, municipal housing, and airport services. The appetite for retaining the best of the past does not change. The glories of the Burrell Collection and the award-winning walkway, opposite the Georgian terraces along the Clyde, are part of to-day's subsidy towards the delight of future generations.

city it was the custom for some unemployed men to spend part of the day in the reading room of the public library and then stroll into the nearby public park to see if there were any duck's eggs they could purloin. The title, ' the hungry thirties ', was devised in other parts of the English-speaking world. Glasgow people, in many cases, were too proud and resourceful ever to use that phrase.

In the ' bad times ' (their standard phrase) they would, if necessary, wring the ducks' necks and eat them at home, without telling anyone.

Towards the end of the 1930s more jobs became available, the tills in the shops rang more frequently. Ship-building output picked up, although to a large extent this was attributable to two ships at Clydebank—first, after a long delay during which the hull lay unfinished on the stocks, the ' Queen Mary '; and, later, her sister ship the ' Queen Elizabeth '. They were the most famous Cunard liners of all.

In 1937 a large industrial estate was built at Hillington, on the outskirts of Glasgow. Two miles away, the British Empire Exhibition was laid out with palaces, pavilions, fountains and piazzas. It brought a stately glamour—and work. There were thousands of visitors from abroad, there was life and colour again. As Glasgow watched the great Exhibition Tower rise from a hilltop in Bellahouston, it could hope that things were looking up at last.

The impact of the war came sharply enough. On September 1, 1939, the Donaldson liner ' Athenia ' left Glasgow with 1000 passengers, mostly women and children who were going to Canada for safety. On September 5, two days after war had been declared, 400 survivors of the U-boat attack which sank her were brought back to the city.

Clydeside's vast industrial machine was thrust from low gear into top gear. Children were evacuated to the country or to the Commonwealth. Mobilisation drafted men and women into the armed forces or to factories, some of which were in other parts of the country where Clydeside skills were needed.

And the bombs came down in the first three years. Glasgow did not suffer to the same extent as Clydebank, Coventry, Plymouth, or, of course, London; but it paid a toll of death and destruction from high-explosives, incendiaries, oil bombs, and parachute mines.

The shipyards built no less than 1549 naval vessels during the war. They also built 354 merchant ships and converted 637 others. People still talk about the amazing feats of endurance and inventiveness that made it possible.

It is typified by the story of how the police had to climb on to the main deck of a ship under construction in the middle of the night to enforce the emergency ' black-out ' regulations by removing a squad of welders who, at their own behest, had decided to work all night so that the ship could be launched on schedule in the morning.

Putting on their guns and their service grey, the Clyde steamers had been back in the battle. They had been to

Dunkirk, as in the First World War, and they had come back fighting in the Normandy invasion. Seven of them were lost between 1939 and 1945.

A man who personified much of the resilient, pawky spirit of Glasgow was Sir Patrick Dollan, Lord Provost during the early part of the war. He was one of the old guard of the I.L.P., a compatriot of Wheatley, Maxton, and the rest. Raised in a mining district in Lanarkshire, he was largely self-taught but he became a politician and leader with an adroit touch for getting the best out of people. He worked prodigiously in raising money for victims of bombing, encouraging the war effort and later planning for the problems of peacetime.

After the war, when the process of renewal began, Scotland's first new town was started at East Kilbride, near Glasgow, and Sir Patrick was to become chairman of its development corporation. People moved out of the city to pleasant, new houses there. A variety of industries (aero engines, electrical goods, textiles etc.) was attracted to it.

Glasgow needed more than that. There was a determination, backed by Labour and Conservative Governments, to tackle at last the removal of the 19th century industrial mess on a grand scale, to give its people living space, and to give its commerce and industry room to manoeuvre in their drive towards new, profitable forms of enterprise.

A world gazetteer, published in America, referred to Glasgow at the time: ' It is far too big for little Scotland. . . . To feed and support Glasgow and supply it with energy to keep its industrial wheels turning, it should have at least 20,000,000 people in the country behind it, not a mere 5,000,000 occasionally industrious Scots '.

Planned ' overspill ' of population began in the 1950s with the objective of eventually re-housing 300,000 people elsewhere. The Corporation also designated 29 areas for comprehensive re-development, starting with Gorbals and the adjacent Hutchesontown for which commissions to design apartment buildings were given to two of Britain's most eminent architects, Sir Basil Spence and Sir Robert Matthew.

A second new town, Cumbernauld and later another, Livingston, were launched in Central Scotland almost exclusively for Glasgow overspill. Agreements were reached with local councils in many parts of Scotland to take in people and industries from the city. Special subsidies were paid. All these arrangements have been generally successful in enabling families to adopt a new life elsewhere; but they have been less effective in inducing industries to transfer from the city.

Shipbuilding declined as foreign nations developed their merchant fleets, more vessels were built abroad, the ever-expanding oil tankers and bulk carriers became larger than most yards in the Glasgow area could accommodate. For these and other reasons, shipping in the port also declined. The trend was downriver to berthage in deeper water in the Firth.

In the early 1970s there was a brief flare-up of the old temper of the city in the successful campaign, complete with fighting funds and banner-waving marches, to prevent the closure of the Upper Clyde shipyards. But the old tag, 'Red Clydeside', was faded and forgotten years before that, except perhaps in sedate, antediluvian men's clubs in faraway cities.

The new Glasgow, in the heart of an area which has been re-stocked with an impressive array of imported industries, making vehicles, earth-moving plant, office machinery and light engineering products, is still changing at a remarkable rate. It has advisedly shed some of its people. It has lost all of its trams, some of its railways, and much of its maritime traffic. It has not lost its powers of adaptability.

Nor has it lost its Scottish proclivity for indulging in superlatives. 'We have the tallest block of flats in Britain. . . . Our motorway programme is the biggest in Britain. . . . The Glasgow-London air service is the busiest in Europe.'

Naturally, it is hungry for more. There are plenty of skills. Strathclyde University (formed out of what was originally Anderson's College, later the Royal College of Science and Technology) has taken its place alongside Glasgow University. The city is one of the foremost centres of the nation for cancer research, bio-engineering, electrical engineering and advanced physics.

One of the finest private art collections in the world is to be given its prescribed place of honour. Sir William Burrell, a former shipowner, presented it to the city in a deed of gift. Items or sections from the collections have been displayed in public from time to time but, because of difficulties in meeting his stipulations about the buildings to house it and the location of these buildings, it has never been exhibited, as he wished, in its majestic totality—paintings, tapestries, sculpture, furnishings and Chinese porcelain of almost inestimable value. There are 22 works by Degas, 17 by Daumier and others by Cezanne, Gaugin, Renoir, Manet, Rembrandt, Velasquez and Memling. The list is magnificent.

At last, the troubled legend of the late Sir William's masterpieces is to come to a happy conclusion. A gallery is to be built in the grounds of Pollok House on the southern fringe of the city. The design was chosen in an international competition for architects, sponsored by Glasgow Corporation. The collection will surprise the world.

And when the visitors come to admire it, what will they make of the city? They will find the most hospitable people in Britain. That much is eternal, constantly attested. They are people with characteristics like the city itself—so surprising in their capacities, so peculiar in renewal and comeback.

The scale of Glasgow's physical renewal, over the past 20 years especially, is evidence of the inherent dynamism of the place. Having stripped off the armour of older heavy industries, it is dressing and stage-setting for a new role, or a series of roles. It is still the economic centrepiece of Scotland. Its increasing commercial and administrative status is conspicuous as Government departments or agencies establish themselves in and around it.

Not since the flint coal and blackband ironstone were discovered as the stuff of Victorian prosperity has Scotland had so much natural wealth within her grasp as now. Extraction of North Sea oil and gas entails the building of rigs and drilling platforms. A big new industry, a 'he-man industry' of the kind that Clydesiders know, is beginning to establish itself on the shores of the Firth of Clyde. Glasgow seems likely to be the regional capital from which it will be served.

The wheel of fortune comes round again. There is all to play for and there never was a more exciting time to be alive.

Glasgow, which arose out of the ancient Kingdom of Strathclyde, now returns to Strathclyde. The title has been revived for the largest of the new regions of Scotland under the re-designed pattern of local government. It is a worthy name, a correct name. The people, the cross-bred people of several tribes, who down the centuries have perpetuated the traits of liberal-thinking enterprise, and adaptability, have kept it worthy. Under the same pattern, the governing of the city itself passes from The Corporation of the City of Glasgow to The City of Glasgow District Council in which the historic title of Lord Provost is preserved for the highest office.

In the beginning there was a church on a bluff above the Molendinar. Around it grew a great city. In its time it was the dominant workshop of the world and with its inherent power of survival it will still turn its skilled hands to any job.

Glasgow can make it—always.